REAWAKENINGS

REAWAKENINGS

Thomas Keating

CROSSROAD • NEW YORK

1992

The Crossroad Publishing Company
370 Lexington Avenue, New York, NY 10017

Printed in the United States of America
Typesetting output: TEXSource, Houston

Library of Congress Cataloging-in-Publication Data

Keating, Thomas.
Reawakenings / Thomas Keating.
p.   cm.
ISBN 0-8245-1149-2
1. Meditations.   I. Title.
BX2182.2.K39   1992
232.9'5 — dc20   91-33855
CIP

CONTENTS

Preface   7

AWAKENING TO THE WORD

1   The First Step   *The Loaves and Fishes*   15

2   Sinking and Rising   *The Storm on the Lake–I*   18

3   Seeing Christ in the Storm   *The Storm on the Lake–II*   20

4   The Sleeping Jesus   *The Storm on the Lake–III*   23

5   The Storm in Us   *The Storm on the Lake–IV*   26

6   Moving Beyond Our Role   *"Who Is My Mother?"*   33

7   A Nonjudgmental Attitude   *The Woman Taken in Adultery*   36

8   Repentance as Reorientation   *The Penitent Woman*   39

9   The Birth of Spiritual Attentiveness   *Mary and Martha*   42

10   Awakening the Spiritual Senses   *The Cured Leper*   45

THE PARABLES

11   Intentionality and Consent   *Parables of the Reign of God–I*   51

12   Discernment   *Parables of the Reign of God–II*   54

13   "Where Are You?"   *The Parable of the Sower*   57

14   Perseverance in Prayer   *The Parable of the Widow and the Judge*   60

CELEBRATIONS OF JESUS' PRESENCE

15   Longing for the Light   *First Sunday of Advent*   65

16   Opening to the Gift   *Fourth Sunday of Advent*   67

17   "So Tiny, So Immense..."   *Christmas*   70

18   Christian Enlightenment   *Epiphany–I*   72

19   The Unfolding of the Light   *Epiphany–II*   75

20   The Wisdom of Paradox   *The Presentation of the Child Jesus*   78

21   The Hidden Life   *The Feast of St. Joseph*   80

22   Jesus, the Light of the World   *Lent–I*   82

23   The Great I AM   *Lent–II*   87

24   The Death of Lazarus   *Lent–III*   94

25   Light from Light   *The Paschal Vigil*   100

26   Being Truly Present   *Pentecost–I*   102

27   The Gift of Counsel   *Pentecost–II*   104

28   The Body of Christ   *The Feast of Corpus Christi*   107

29   The Double Bind   *The Feast of St. John the Baptist*   110

30   The Holy Mountain   *The Transfiguration–I*   116

31   Sleepers, Awake!   *The Transfiguration–II*   121

32   Resting in God   *The Transfiguration–III*   125

33   The Resolution of Opposites   *The Transfiguration–IV*   128

PREFACE

At the conclusion of the dialogue between Jesus and the woman at the well, the woman said to him, "I know that Messiah — that is, Christ — is coming, and when he comes he will explain everything." Jesus said, "That is who I am, I who speak to you" (John 4:26).

Jesus repeats these same words to Christians today — and with the same challenge to deepen our understanding and our faith. At first the woman at the well didn't understand what in the world he was talking about, but in the course of their conversation Jesus led her deeper and deeper within herself, to her own deepest yearning for living water, until she was able to take the quantum leap of surrender that we call faith. She then proclaimed his power and goodness to her countrymen and women. Her excitement and joy spilled over onto other people. This is a paradigm of how evangelization is supposed to take place: through personal experience. Without personal experience, what is there to share? One can fill the world with words, but without the experience of what they mean, they are mostly hot air. They simply contribute to the greenhouse effect now taking place for other reasons.

The spiritual journey is an awakening to the words of Christ at an ever-deepening level, which will transform our being. Our tradition provides three interlocking pieces to do so, all grounded in the words of scripture but inviting us to move beyond, from words to Word: God incarnate at the inmost center of our being.

The first interlocking piece is *lectio divina*, which might be paraphrased as *"listening* (with our hearts, not just our minds) to the texts we believe to be divinely inspired." *Lectio divina* is the most traditional way of cultivating the dialogue with Christ. It is a way of listening to the texts of scripture as if we were in conversation with Christ and he were suggesting the topics of conversation. The daily encounter with Christ and reflection on his word leads beyond mere acquaintanceship to an attitude of friendship, trust, and love. Conversation simplifies and gives way to communing, or as Gregory the Great (sixth century), summarizing the Christian contemplative tradition, put it, "resting in God."

The second interlocking piece is the practice of contemplative prayer. Contemplative prayer is the normal development of the grace of baptism and the regular practice of *lectio divina*. We may think of prayer as thoughts or feelings expressed in words. But this is only one expression. Contemplative prayer is the opening of mind and heart — our whole being — to God, the Ultimate Mystery, beyond thoughts, words, and emotions. We open our awareness to God whom we know by faith is within us, closer than breathing, closer than thinking, closer than consciousness itself. Contemplative prayer is a process of interior purification leading, if we consent, to divine union. Although in recent centuries viewed with suspicion as a special grace conferred upon only a chosen few, contemplative prayer has now been restored as the baptismal gift of every Christian, and modern methods such as Centering Prayer present the church's contemplative heritage in an updated and accessible form.

The third interlocking piece is the liturgy. This book focuses primarily on the awakenings to the word of God that take place through the liturgy. The following chapters are homilies presented at the Eucharist over the past two liturgical years. I call this book *Reawakenings* because it builds on the reflections of an earlier series of homilies, called *Awakenings*, and because the water that Jesus provides is "a spring...welling up for eternal life" (John 4:14). Through the inspiration of the Holy Spirit, whose constant flowing movement the spring of water symbolizes, there are awakenings and reawakenings as new depths of meaning unfold in the texts of scripture.

The liturgy is not merely a celebration of historical events. In the perspective of the liturgy, grace is the presence and action of Christ in our lives right now. The same grace offered throughout the Gospel in particular teachings and events is presented day after day in the celebration of the Eucharist. Christ lives in the hearts of the faithful, especially when they are gathered together in his name.

The liturgy gathers the incidents of Christ's life around the great theological themes of divine light, life, and love. Light is the theme of Advent, Christmas, and Epiphany. In that season the great theme of divine light is looked at from the perspective of preparation, celebration, and follow-up. The transmission of the divine light prepared for by Advent and received at Christmas, is celebrated in the festal season of Epiphany.

Lent deals with the next theological idea, namely, divine life. It is the preparation for the celebration of divine life. Holy Week and Easter are the principal feasts. Then in the Sundays after Easter we are led to understand what has been communicated, like slowly unpacking Christmas presents in order to appreciate them more fully. The Ascension is the crowning feast of the divine life in us.

The liturgy, then, is an extraordinary production in which the church tries to make available to our senses, imagination, reasoning, and reflection, the heart of the Gospel, which is the transmission of divine life: not the memory of it, not the knowledge of it, but the *experience* of it. And not any experience of it, but rather Christ's experience of the Ultimate Reality as Abba, the God of infinite compassion and concern for every living thing, especially people.

Perhaps it would make this truth graphic for us if we compared the experience of the liturgical events to a television documentary. In this comparison the screen is not outside us but is the inner screen of consciousness, and this documentary is not pre-recorded, even though it deals with historical events; it is a live program that is taking place within us right now. No television program compares with this aspect of the liturgy. The show is taking place not just in our living room, but in us. It is an immanent and intimate communication that is not only live and happening now, but happening within us.

Faith, of course, is active on different levels. We might compare faith working through reason to a black and white picture. As our receptive apparatus improves, like the advent of color television, the picture becomes more engaging. This corresponds to the fruits of the Spirit in which we move beyond the limitations of rational reflection and begin to touch God or, rather, God touches us with more intimate and direct communications. The television industry is now developing a high-definition picture in which the images will be vastly improved and all the colors sharply differentiated. This kind of receptivity might correspond to the empowerment of the Beatitudes. In any case, there is a progression in our receptive capacity. God's self-disclosure remains the same, but we receive it according to our capacity.

The process of *lectio divina* follows the same kind of progression, incidentally. *Lectio divina* is a method of refining our receptive apparatus. The fourth stage of *lectio divina*, which is contemplative prayer, is a new dimension that goes on refining itself and improving. We might compare contemplative prayer to high-definition TV in which the reception is clearer than in real life.

As one's receptivity improves and the picture becomes more perfect, the transmission of the meaning of Christ's life and message becomes more available. Clarity of understanding rather than clarity of form or image is the purpose of this transmission. Its ultimate purpose is purity of intention, or what the Fathers of the Desert called "purity of heart." The purification of the will from the false self and its self-centered motivation enables the transmission to take place without static or the distortion of the message. What we perceive is not a picture, but the undifferentiated presence of God. The God of faith and love *is* the transmission. As these communications unfold, our faculties respond with different levels of absorption in the divine presence. St. Teresa of Avila describes them in *The Interior Castle* as the stages of interior prayer. These are our human responses to the divine life within us. When our senses, imagination, memory, intuitive faculties, and spiritual sensitivities are activated and refined, they tend to react to the divine life, light, and love with experiences of the divine presence on various levels of absorption. The divine transmission, however, is present without our interpretation, and this is its most profound meaning.

In other religions there is a transmission that an enlightened guru can communicate to the disciple. In Christianity there is a charismatic gift called "slaying in the Spirit" in which a similar kind of inner experience can be evoked by certain gifted healers. We might debate the relative depth of these different experiences, but they all involve at least some transmission. The transmission of Christ in the liturgy transcends transient experience and the whole range of our faculties. The invisible rays that fill the universe are not immediately apparent to us; it is only with an instrument that we can translate them into knowledge. Similarly, the divine transmission is communication in its purest form. As we sit before this mysterious television set within and watch a screen in which there is no thought, no particular object, but only the general loving presence of God, and as this attention becomes pure intention, we open ourselves to the fullest meaning of the liturgy, in its ever-deepening cycles, which is to receive the divine life and to be transformed, not into some extraordinary personage, but into an ordinary human being with extraordinary love.

ACKNOWLEDGMENTS

Special thanks to Patricia Johnson, Bonnie Shimizu, and Cynthia Bourgeault for editorial assistance and to the many retreat groups whose presence and prayer inspired these reflections.

AWAKENING TO THE WORD

1

THE FIRST STEP

After this, Jesus went across the Sea of Galilee [of Tiberias]. A large crowd followed him, because they saw the signs he was performing on the sick. Jesus went up on the mountain, and there he sat down with his disciples. The Jewish feast of Passover was near. When Jesus raised his eyes and saw that a large crowd was coming to him, he said to Philip, "Where can we buy enough food for them to eat?" He said this to test him, because he himself knew what he was going to do. Philip answered him, "Two hundred days' wages worth of food would not be enough for each of them to have a little [bit]." One of his disciples, Andrew, the brother of Simon Peter, said to him, "There is a boy here who has five barley loaves and two fish; but what good are these for so many?" Jesus said, "Have the people recline." Now there was a great deal of grass in that place. So the men reclined, about five thousand in number. Then Jesus took the loaves, gave thanks, and distributed them to those who were reclining, and also as much of the fish as they wanted. When they had had their fill, he said to his disciples, "Gather the fragments left over, so that nothing will be wasted." So they collected them, and filled twelve wicker baskets with fragments from the five barley loaves that had been more than they could eat. When the people saw the sign he had done, they said, "This is truly the Prophet, the one who is to come into the world." Since Jesus knew that they were going to come and carry

him off to make him king, he withdrew again to the mountain
alone. (John 6:1–15)

Jesus approaches this impossible situation with ease because he
knows that nothing is impossible with God. He knows the divine
goodness will find a way out.

The feast of the Passover was near. The Passover was the annual
celebration that brought people from all over Israel on a three- or
four-day journey to Jerusalem to celebrate the commemoration of
the liberation from Egypt and the coming to the promised land.
Many of these pilgrims were fascinated by Jesus and enthralled
by his miracles. They joined with the local peasantry in following
him into the desert and up the mountainside. At the end of the day
he found a vast throng of tired and hungry people with no local
concession stands of any kind to take care of their needs. Jesus said
to Philip, "What shall we do?" Philip replied, "There is not enough
to give everybody even a mouthful."

Jesus answered, "Have them all sit down." Soon the enormous
crowd was sitting on the grass waiting to be fed. Available were
two dried fish and five barley loaves for about thirty thousand
people (including women and children). What did Jesus do? What
I suggest is not the usual interpretation, but might be acceptable
as a reinterpretation to suggest an even greater miracle. He took
one step, and then stepped back and let God do the rest. What was
that step? It was the extraordinary gesture of attempting to feed
thousands of people with next to nothing. Jesus blessed the bread
and fishes and handed them to the disciples to pass around. That
gesture of confidence opened the hearts of the people. Those who
had come from nearby had nothing to share. Others had supplies
they had brought with them for their four-day stay in Jerusalem.
When they saw Jesus make this extraordinary act of confidence in
them, they reached into their haversacks and pulled out all that
was there. As they passed around their supplies, everybody had
more than was needed. Twelve baskets of food were left over.

The greatest miracle is the opening of the human heart to the
generosity of God. The first step in responding to human need does
not have to be a big thing, but it may change the world. Jesus with

absolute confidence passed out the few crumbs that were available and let God do the rest. He touched just the right chord in people's hearts and all the doors opened.

In every desperate situation, somebody has to take the first step, some action that the Creator can turn into a channel of grace; once it has been taken, the divine energy can flow and provide a superabundance of what is needed.

When Mother Teresa picked up a dying man in the streets of Calcutta, she captured the imagination of the world. It was a striking symbol of God's concern for the poor. Each of us is surrounded by opportunities. We don't have to be invited to the United Nations or go to a summit conference to save the world. Divine love suggests a first step that needs to be taken here and now. If we respond, the initial effects may not be much, but in due time the results may reach beyond our wildest expectations.

Quantum physics tells us that a single thought changes the universe. This is an insight into what the mystics have always understood. Divine love has to manifest itself. It waits for us to give its immense energy an occasion to flow. When the people saw the miracle, they wanted to make Jesus a king. He did not have the slightest interest in being a king. He fled into the mountain because he was sent to manifest love, not political ambition. He would not do what he was not sent to do. He was sent to manifest what he saw the Father doing. This is to show love without limit and to awaken others to its presence in them.

2

SINKING AND RISING

Then he made the disciples get into the boat and precede him to the other side, while he dismissed the crowds. After doing so, he went up on the mountain by himself to pray. When it was evening he was there alone. Meanwhile the boat, already a few miles offshore, was being tossed about by the waves, for the wind was against it. During the fourth watch of the night, he came toward them, walking on the sea. When the disciples saw him walking on the sea they were terrified. "It is a ghost," they said, and they cried out in fear. At once [Jesus] spoke to them. "Take courage, it is I; do not be afraid." Peter said to him in reply, "Lord, if it is you, command me to come to you on the water." He said, "Come." Peter got out of the boat and began to walk on the water toward Jesus. But when he saw how [strong] the wind was he became frightened; and, beginning to sink, he cried out, "Lord, save me!" Immediately Jesus stretched out his hand and caught him, and said to him, "O you of little faith, why did you doubt?" After they got into the boat, the wind died down. Those who were in the boat did him homage, saying, "Truly, you are the Son of God." (Matthew 14:22–33)

This event follows the miraculous multiplication of the loaves and fishes. After the crowd dispersed, Jesus directed the disciples to make passage by boat to the opposite shore while he went up the mountain to pray. As he prayed, a storm came up on the lake. Moved by his sensitivity and concern, he decided to see how the disciples were doing and started coming to them, walking on the water. It was three o'clock in the morning. The disciples thought he was a ghost. They cried out in fear. He tried to reassure them: "It is only me."

Jesus emerging from the winds and the waves is the symbol that he is present *in* the wind and the waves. The problem with the disciples was that they didn't expect Jesus to come to them out of this or any other storm; hence, they perceived the one who was right in front of their eyes as something else, a ghost.

Peter yelled out, "Lord, if it is you, let me come to you over the water!" Jesus held out his arms saying, "Come!" Peter started to walk on the water, his eyes fixed on Jesus. Suddenly a big wave splashed against Peter's legs and the spray lashed his face. His focus began to waver. It shifted from Jesus to the waves, and he began to sink. He cried out, "Lord, save me!" Jesus reached out and pulled him from the water. Immediately the storm subsided, and all acknowledged Jesus as the Son of God.

We, also, experience the wind and the waves. Even when we recognize Jesus, our initial trust begins to waver when things get rough. Our focus shifts, and we begin to sink. Jesus remains patient. He gives us relief for a while, and then once again another storm arises. We try, we fail, we sink. If we call for help, he rescues us and gives us a breather. Then the cycle starts over: the storm, the initial burst of trust, the wind and the waves, doubts, the sinking. The chief things to worry about are sinking without calling out for help, or going ashore and staying there. Peter deserves credit because he risked a lot while the others stayed in the boat. He also deserves credit for his response to failure. When the wind and the waves got to him, he knew how to call for help. The biggest danger in the spiritual journey is not to take any risk. We may think the spiritual journey is a magic carpet to bliss. It is rather the humiliation of the false self. This is the formation that Jesus gave to his first disciples. We can be sure that his contemporary disciples are much the same, and so is he. Accordingly, one description of a disciple might be this: always trying, always failing, always trying again.

3

SEEING CHRIST IN THE STORM

*Then he made his disciples get into the boat and precede him to
the other side toward Bethsaida, while he dismissed the crowd.
And when he had taken leave of them, he went off to the mountain to pray. When it was evening, the boat was far out on the
sea and he was alone on the shore. Then he saw that they were
tossed about while rowing, for the wind was against them. About
the fourth watch of the night, he came toward them walking on
the sea. He meant to pass by them. But when they saw him walking on the sea, they thought it was a ghost and cried out. They
had all seen him and were terrified. But at once he spoke with
them, "Take courage, it is I, do not be afraid!" He got into the
boat with them and the wind died down. They were [completely]
astounded. They had not understood the incident of the loaves.
On the contrary, their hearts were hardened.* (Mark 6:45–52)

"They had not understood the incident of the loaves. On the
contrary, their hearts were hardened." This is a perfect description
of our lack of perceiving God in everyday life. It is hard for us to
find God in the middle of the stuff we call daily life — hard to find
God in it, with it, through it, and beyond it. These four ways of
perceiving God's presence are primary objectives of the grace of
Christ, which, sense by sense and faculty by faculty, refines our capacity to receive, so that our awareness may tune in and resonate
with God's more profound communications. The permanent trans-

formation of our entire nature is the divine project, not just a few extraordinary but temporary graces.

Daily life in spiritual literature is called by various names: a desert, forest, ocean, prairie — an endless expanse of ever-recurring duties, failures, and difficulties spreading out in every direction. We seem to be getting nowhere not only fast, but ever more slowly. This sense of getting nowhere is the place to which contemplative prayer brings us. The x-ray eyes of faith have not yet become sufficiently penetrating to perceive the content of daily life and our ordinary commitments as unlimited possibilities for growth and transformation.

The apostles were just as dense as we are and maybe more so. They did not understand that Jesus had perceived the presence of God in the hunger of the great crowd following him. God was feeding the multitude, just as in the liturgy he feeds us. Same God, same grace, same basic congregation — the same sort of people who cannot or will not see the presence of God in ordinary circumstances. We want to see God in cathedrals with huge choirs, solemn processions, clouds of incense, banks of candles, and pipe organs blasting away. God, of course, is there, too. But God is also present in changing diapers; God is right there in every human activity.

The mountain is the symbol of interior solitude. Like Moses and Elijah and the other prophets, Jesus withdrew into solitude from time to time to be with the Father and to access to the full the divine energy that was always with him. This energy sustains the universe; it sustains us. It becomes more accessible as we open to the divine life within us.

Jesus manifests the need of human beings to withdraw from time to time; not necessarily externally — that is the symbol — but into the inner mountain of solitude and silence. Solitude is the means of detachment and submission to God's will. In this incident Jesus, having saturated himself in the atmosphere of the divine, emerges into action and starts walking on the water.

Notice how Jesus constantly reminds us that he is manifesting the Father. He says, "I do nothing except what I see the Father doing." Jesus gives not only himself to us, but the Father.

Jesus sees the disciples tossed around by the wind and the waves and is moved by the Father's concern. The divine energy can do anything once it has been accessed, so walking on the water is no difficulty. The disciples see Jesus emerging out of the winds and the waves, and they are terrified. They cry out, "It's a ghost!" The text states that Jesus meant to pass by them, suggesting that if they had not called out, he would have gone on. Why? Because they were not seeing him in the immediate situation. Jesus also comes down our streets and into the events of our lives, and unless we are alert, he may pass by. If we are scared, like the disciples, we can at least shout for help! If we express our need, he rescues us from the difficulties that we get into day after day.

The text says that the disciples did not understand either the multiplication of the loaves or what happened on the lake. The wind and the waves are symbols of affliction, difficulty, and confusion. In other words, the disciples did not recognize Jesus in the storm. He had to tell them, "It is I, not a ghost."

Every time we find life, people, or events blowing us away and we are rowing like mad and getting nowhere, Christ is inviting us to perceive him in the situation. This does not mean merely to resign ourselves to the trial. This is the first movement. Grace not only moves us to accept every situation, but may also move us to do something about our situation: to correct or improve it in some way. Grace enhances our capacity not only to see Christ in every situation and to accept him, but to do what he would do. It is the freedom to allow things to be just as they are or to act — and to know which response is appropriate.

4

THE SLEEPING JESUS

On that day, as evening drew on, he said to them, "Let us cross to the other side." Leaving the crowd, they took him with them in the boat just as he was. And other boats were with him. A violent squall came up and waves were breaking over the boat, so that it was already filling up. Jesus was in the stern, asleep on a cushion. They woke him and said to him, "Teacher, do you not care that we are perishing?" He woke up, rebuked the wind, and said to the sea, "Quiet! Be still!" The wind ceased and there was great calm. Then he asked them, "Why are you so terrified? Do you not yet have faith?" They were filled with great awe and said to one another, "Who then is this whom even wind and sea obey?" (Mark 4:35–41)

This event mirrors our personal experience in the spiritual journey when we are flooded with difficulties and trials — a familiar experience for those practicing contemplative prayer. Every now and then we hit a bad squall and spend the time of prayer bailing out our sinking boat. Sometimes we get frantic and can't even find the sacred word; it's buried under the wind and the waves. We cry out, "Help!" *Help* is one of the greatest prayers ever composed. It is short, to the point, and effective. As fast as we bail out our discomforting thoughts, others flow back in. If we have preconceived ideas or expectations that contemplative prayer will lead us to a state of no thoughts or to the intimate presence of God, the storms can get frightening. When the winds and waves are overwhelming, the question arises, "I thought that Jesus would be here . . . but if he is, he must be fast asleep."

In this incident Jesus was not only asleep but sleeping on a cushion, thus adding insult to injury. He was very comfortable and not the least bit disturbed by the storm. When the disciples reached the end of their rope, they woke him up. "Don't you care that we are going down?" they cried out. Jesus got up and rebuked the wind and the storm saying, "Be still."

These words must resonate in those who are veterans of contemplative prayer. Think of them each time your prayer is dry as dust or you find yourself bombarded with thoughts, struggling with boredom, or utterly discouraged; or when you think that God has gone on a trip to the outer confines of the cosmos, or that God doesn't care about you anymore. This is one of the most frequent projections that people fall into when they are discouraged. Commentaries multiply like, "I must have done something wrong," or "Maybe I'm not doing this right." The afflictive emotions may be reinforced by commentaries from our personal history such as "Nobody loves me. I always ruin everything" — and on and on.

The Lord responds to our desperate cry for help as he did to the disciples. All of a sudden, without knowing how it happened, a delicious peace descends upon us as if we were enveloped in a kind of embrace. We feel ashamed that we ever doubted God's love or presence. It is as if Jesus said in the midst of our turmoil, "My peace I give you." Or to the storm, "Be still."

When God says, "Be still," everything is still. Whatever God says happens instantly.

Why did the disciples wake Jesus up? Because they were scared. A further question: Was it necessary to wake him up? It would seem not, because Jesus immediately asked, "Why were you terrified?" Through events, other people, and our experience of prayer, these precise questions are directed to us as we practice contemplative prayer. We go through periods of turmoil, get frightened, wake Jesus up, experience the wonderful calm he bestows, and are reassured. Suppose we hadn't woke him up? Would we have been protected? Of course! That is the point of the story. Jesus is present in every storm. Since his protection is always present, there is nothing to be afraid of.

Then he asks a further question, "Where is your faith?" We wake him up because we don't believe he is present. We don't believe he is helping us in secret. If we are expecting God to heal us and it doesn't happen on a conscious level, that does not mean that God is not healing us on another level. In fact, God's lack of help on one level is the way God moves us from one level of faith to another level. In other words, if God responds to us where we want him to respond, like the disciples who wanted Jesus to start bailing to get the water out of the boat, we may never find out that God's help is always available at a deeper level. The divine assistance is never missing no matter what the storm, no matter what we may feel or think. We regularly project our psychological experience onto Christ and experience him as not caring for us: he seems to be sleeping. We have a choice whether to wake him up or let him have a good snooze. At one level of faith, we panic and yell for help, but if we move to the mature faith to which contemplative prayer leads us, we have misgivings about waking him up. We may even say to ourselves, "He's helping me anyway." Then we are really making some headway in the spiritual journey. Our trust in God is expanding.

Once we believe that God is present in the storm and is protecting us, we know we have all the help we need. God never goes anywhere; he just seems to. Sometimes God takes a lengthy snooze and seems quite content to sleep on and leave us in our anxiety. The purpose of God's sleeping is to make us realize that he has not left us at all, but is assisting us more than ever at a deeper, more subtle level. This is the level of pure faith. The conviction grows that whatever we may feel or think, Jesus is in our little boat and is giving us all the help we need; we can just relax and let go of all fear.

5

THE STORM IN US

On that day, as evening drew on, he said to them, "Let us cross to the other side." Leaving the crowd, they took him with them in the boat just as he was. And other boats were with him. A violent squall came up and waves were breaking over the boat, so that it was already filling up. Jesus was in the stern, asleep on a cushion. They woke him and said to him, "Teacher, do you not care that we are perishing?" He woke up, rebuked the wind, and said to the sea, "Quiet! Be still!" The wind ceased and there was great calm. Then he asked them, "Why are you so terrified? Do you not yet have faith?" They were filled with great awe and said to one another, "Who then is this whom even wind and sea obey?" (Mark 4:35–41)

Contemplative prayer is a movement of faith. Our varied experiences are an essential part of the growing process. This mysterious education consists in the Spirit training us to trust God. When we have a prolonged period of dryness in prayer, our former practices of spiritual reading and the liturgy normally dry out, too. All benefit seems to drain out of every spiritual exercise and prayer is hard, grinding work. Nothing seems to help. We are tempted to think that we have done something wrong. We may be wedded to our expectation that the spiritual nourishment we had enjoyed is going to remain at banquet level for the rest of our lives. It isn't. The diet changes. The food that nourished us in the beginning of our spiritual journey becomes insipid and does not nourish anymore.

This is because the nourishment came from God's grace, and God has withdrawn it in order to invite us to a deeper level of faith and more substantial spiritual food. Since we have not yet experienced this new level of faith and its benefits, we do not know that it is an option. We think the only option is to forget about prayer and try to get to heaven some other way. Of course, this doesn't work.

In this text, Jesus is dealing with the exact problem that we have been describing. The disciples don't know about this new level of faith. Hence they interpret Jesus' presence when he is not doing what they expect him to do as a lack of concern. But Jesus is simply present in a new way that only a new level of faith can access. God never leaves us. God could not leave us or we would just dissolve into a grease spot. God is creating us at every microcosmic moment of time or we wouldn't be here. The divine creative action sustains us on every level of our being. The spiritual journey is about trying to get our conscious life in harmony with the divine action. This is a process that leads step by step to deeper levels of union.

The only way to get from one level to the next level is to move. Since we only know the level we are on, we are reluctant to move. We even get annoyed and conjure up commentaries that make matters worse. All one has to do in the storm is to persevere in prayer, trust, and wait it out. God is at a new level and we are still at the old one. Naturally God seems to have gone. God has gone from the place he used to be to a new place and is waiting for us to join him at that level. The problem is that we haven't gone to the level where God is. The way to pass from here to there is to exercise patience during the transition and confidence in God's unfailing assistance no matter what the difficulties, whether they come from outside or from inside. God is waiting for us and if we are quiet, we may even hear him "snoring." When we hear God snoring, we can find our way to where God is. Once the transition has been made, our union with God will be reinforced. The disciples were amazed and greatly strengthened in faith when he stood up and said to the wind and the waves, "Be still," and a great calm descended.

The same thing happens to us when we are in a storm and call out to the Lord and he responds to our cries for help. All of a sudden there is a great calm. How close God is! How well God knows exactly what we are going through. And how much God sympathizes and wants to help. But if God helps too soon, we may bog down where we are, or even regress to a less mature level of faith. God is trying to move us to the deepest level where he can fill us to the maximum with the divine life. We must not misunderstand God's intention in this process.

In this vignette, we see that the Spirit is speaking to our condition now, especially as we enter contemplative prayer and submit to God's healing work within us, which I like to refer to as "the divine therapy." Jesus is waiting for us at a new level where faith is purer and our capacity for divine love is expanded. It is essential for our growth that we get out of where we are with our expectations and live without them. I don't want to diminish how disconcerting and confusing this period is. The first thing we need is to determine the diagnosis. Why are we upset? That is what Jesus wanted to know when he asked the disciples, "Why are you afraid?" The answer is that we are still under the influence of our emotional programs and our value systems in the unconscious that place an emotional judgment on our interior states. The emotions have no way of knowing what is good and what isn't good for the whole person. They only report what they feel. They simply record what feels good or not good. This is not the kind of judgment that is suitable for adults. It belongs to children who have a habit of going with their feelings. We have to be weaned from our emotional judgment that trials are a disaster, that dryness is the worst thing that can happen to us, that boredom is unbearable, or that we must have consolation in order to pursue the spiritual journey. Suppose we could be detached from such things; what would happen? We would experience this new level right away. The habit of doubting what the divine therapist is doing prevents us from submitting, and hence we have to go through a number of trials in order to see the profound wisdom of the process.

The divine therapy is healing the emotional wounds of early childhood and the programs we developed to cope with those wounds. The value system in the unconscious wants security symbols, power and control over others, affection, esteem, and pleasure as guarantees of happiness. There is nothing wrong with these instinctual needs as human values, but they are not substitutes for God. The Gospel is an invitation to change the direction in which we are looking for happiness, not only consciously but unconsciously. The false values continue to live in the unconscious even after we have consciously decided to change them. The discipline of contemplative prayer is part of the dynamic of dismantling the value systems in the unconscious. When values are unconscious, that means that we are not aware of them. Furthermore, because we developed these programs for happiness in early childhood, there is no limit or moderation to them. Hence no one on earth could achieve happiness through the pursuit of them. At the very least we are in competition with everyone else in the human family since they, too, are in desperate search for the same objectives.

The Gospel calls us out of that childishness into full personal responsibility for our emotions. Contemplative prayer demolishes the monumental illusion that God is absent. As we enter contemplative prayer, we move toward a certain level of rest and peace. In the beginning it is hard to develop the habit of letting go of our ordinary train of thoughts promptly, but little by little we feel the attraction to be still. We may even enjoy a few moments of rest. That rest is the rest to which Jesus invited everyone who is heavily burdened. "Come to me all you who are heavily burdened and I will give you rest." As rest is experienced, our emotional judgment says, "This is great! At last I am getting somewhere! Maybe it was worthwhile after all." Precisely because we have experienced some rest, the defense mechanisms that keep the repressed material in the unconscious relax. When we repress emotional experiences in early childhood, the emotional energy does not go away; it is stored in the body where it blocks the free flow of the natural energies and grace. It can make us physically sick; it also places us at a psychological disadvantage. The best thing that can happen to us is to have this undigested emotional material removed. It does harm by remaining in the body, like a meal that we did not digest.

Thus, the divine therapy, through the deep rest accessed in times of contemplative prayer, loosens up the hardpan around the emotional weeds of a lifetime, and the unconscious begins to unload. As a result, we have a bombardment of thoughts with an emotional charge to them and sometimes raw emotions like anger or fear. To repress such thoughts is like pushing vomit back into our stomach when it is on the way up. If we let it go, we will feel much better. That is why the method of centering prayer tells us not to resist thoughts. Thoughts and rest are two sides of the same process. They are part of the same circular motion. As soon as we evacuate some emotional junk, the grace of God fills that space. Thoughts and rest are essential to the process until we come to the bottom of the pile of junk. When that happens, we are in divine union.

We need to develop confidence in the process. It is like descending a spiral staircase. Until we get to the bottom, we keep recycling the same emotional problems or temptations, but not on the same level. So we say, "Here I am again, the same old stick. I'm angry again after a whole year of good feelings. I'm having the same temptations I thought were solved ten years ago." Well, they *were* solved, but only up to a point and on one level. The divine action is now inviting us to let go of them at a much deeper level. Thus, we recycle what seems to be the same old problems on the horizontal plane, but vertically we are handling them in a much more mature and substantial way, which in turn will enable us to yield ourselves to the divine action more completely.

We learn to trust God by the experience of God's reliability in these storms. Eventually we are convinced that the storm is not a sign that God has gone away, but rather, God has moved to a deeper level of our consciousness where he is inviting us to join him.

When thoughts and feelings are coming from the unconscious, they bear no relationship to anything we can remember in the recent past. That is a sure sign we are getting in touch with something in early childhood that was never adequately processed and has been sitting there for twenty, thirty, or forty years. If we can unload it, we will experience a great sense of wellbeing.

We need to take a positive view of this process. It is like an archaeological dig. Archaeologists working in the Near East excavate big mounds called "tells." In ancient times, when the victors burned down a conquered town, they built a new one on top of the old. As the rubble accumulated, the tells grew higher and higher. Thus, centuries of successive civilizations can all be found in one place. The archaeologists start at the top and clean off what is there: rubbish, broken shards, ashes. They throw out the junk and send the mosaics to a museum. Then they take a vacation, enjoy these works of art, and come back the next spring to dig for the next civilization. In this manner they work down to the Stone Age.

The Holy Spirit seems to follow the same kind of methodology. The following scenario is a frequent one: The divine action picks us up where we are now. During the period of our conversion, the Spirit cleans up a few of our compulsions and relationships so we can enjoy life a little more. We experience a newfound sense of freedom and a certain enthusiasm for spiritual things. After a little while, the Spirit decides to work through the whole of our personal history period by period. The Spirit starts out with our adult life and cleans that up, preserving all that was good and throwing out the junk. We feel better, enjoy another plateau. Then the Spirit comes back for another dig and our adolescence is worked over. As we near the bottom of the pile — puberty, early childhood, infancy, or the womb — the emotions become more primitive. The bio-computer of the brain remembers painful incidents just as we first felt them. We experience the very feelings we had when we felt neglected, abandoned, or unloved at age one week, one month, or one year. In general, every time this dig moves to a deeper level of the unconscious, we think we are getting worse. We are not getting worse; we are simply coming to the bottom of the pile of emotional debris. When we finally reach the bottom, we are in transforming union and the inner resurrection under the guidance of the Spirit begins. Daily life under the influence of the Spirit becomes a continuous exercise of love.

It is only after the Spirit works through much of the junk that we can live the fruits of the Spirit and the Beatitudes. Although the evacuation of the unconsciousness takes place primarily during the period of contemplative prayer, the emotions may continue to evacuate outside the time of prayer. For example, we may notice an intense reaction to a situation or person that normally would not bother us at all. A childhood feeling loosened by the deep rest of contemplation is coming to consciousness and makes use of this event as a means to evacuate the painful feeling. The intensity

of the childhood feeling is evoked by the event or person that
has some similarity to the original traumatic experience. Thus, the
event serves as a catalyst, a way of evacuating an emotion that was
not completely unloaded during the time of prayer.

"Why are you afraid?" That is Jesus' question to us as well
as to his disciples in the boat. Through events and during prayer
he is continually asking, "What is your motivation?" If we can
identify our hidden motives, they are the reason we are afraid. If
we change the value system in the unconscious, we won't be afraid
of anything. Peace flows from the conviction of our rootedness in
God, a presence of infinite concern and caring. Then the winds and
waves can no longer disturb us.

6

MOVING BEYOND OUR ROLE

While he was still speaking to the crowds, his mother and his brothers appeared outside, wishing to speak with him. [Someone told him, "Your mother and your brothers are standing outside, asking to speak with you."] But he said in reply to the one who told him, "Who is my mother? Who are my brothers?" And stretching out his hand toward his disciples, he said, "Here are my mother and my brothers. For whoever does the will of my heavenly Father is my brother, and sister, and mother." (Matthew 12:46–49)

Jesus' mother and brothers come for a family visit and see to get the ear of the teacher. Jesus seems unwilling to give then any time. His response to their request is a question: "Who ar my mother, brothers, and sisters?" Then he points to the disciple: Are we to understand by his example that we should disregard th reasonable requests of parents and loved ones for a few minutes of our time? His seeming rudeness seems rather to be parable in action.

Jesus uses the occasion to warn his disciples about playing a role. This precaution is not the same as to have no role. It is rather an exhortation not to overidentify with one's role, not to be sucked into the fascination of overidentification with one's group. The need for acceptance by family or peers tends to shape our self-image and thus prevents us from actually fulfilling our role. The spiritual journey involves the sifting not only of our motivation, but the liberation from our self-image and worldview insofar as they hinder our response to the will of God. In this text, Jesus shocks his disciples into the awareness that even the role of being his mother has a limited significance. We enter fully into our vocation only by being willing not to be whatever we are! By this statement, I do not mean to imply that we can disregard the duties of our role but that we should not take a possessive attitude toward them.

If you are a mother, you naturally want to fulfil your motherly role. But this does not mean that your children must live up to your expectations, and still less fulfill your own unconscious needs that were never fulfilled. "They're *my* children. Although they are now over forty, I must still try to get them into the profession I want them to be in or involve myself in their divorce."

If a husband perceives himself as macho, he may feel he has to dominate or overprotect his family to feel like a real man. As for children, how hard it is for them to break the roles that dysfunctional families have imposed on them. They tend to repeat the same mistakes that their parents made in their upbringing.

Our Blessed Mother was not offended by Jesus' apparent disregard of her role as his mother. She had already been through the "de-role-ing" process. She had understood that God's will for her was a life of virginity. Then without any prior explanation an angel said, "God wants you to be a mother." What would an ordinary girl think about that? Her first thought was certainly not, "I will have a virgin birth." Such an event had never happened before. On the contrary, she naturally thought, "It's the end. My certainty about God's will for me must be wrong. I guess I never really knew God's will. I just thought I did."

The statement that she was to be a mother was a bomb shattering her carefully laid plans. Her confidence in discerning God's will was pulled out from under her. Her response was to seek more information. "How can this be since I have made a commitment not to enter a conjugal relationship?" Her question is the key to resolving apparent contradictions. God does not necessarily want us to give up our role or our lifestyle. God wants us to give up our possessive attitude toward it, because that is what hinders the will of God from unfolding.

According to Jesus, John the Baptist was the greatest man born of woman. His prophetic role was to point out the Messiah. Why then did he send disciples to Jesus to say, "Are you the Messiah or are we waiting for somebody else?" Was this incredibly holy man wondering whether he had pointed out the wrong person?

Jesus may not have fit John's preconceived ideas regarding the Messiah. John was an ascetic; Jesus was not. John's disciples fasted; Jesus' did not. His disciples kept the Law; Jesus' did not. In fact, Jesus disregarded many of the customs of the rabbis. He taught along the road; rabbis preached only in synagogues. He rarely referred to scripture; they based their whole teaching on it. Rabbis did not speak to women in public; he spoke to women freely and made friends with them. People stuck in role models are careful to observe the rules and to conform to social expectations; they prefer the law to people.

Perhaps John, because of his overidentification with his ascetical ideal, may have been tempted in his last days to think, "Is Jesus of Nazareth really the Messiah?" If such a doubt was gnawing at him, it would have led him to ask the further question, "Do I have an obligation in conscience to correct my mistake?" Thus, John's suffering in prison, perhaps in a state of depression, provided the occasion for the ultimate doubt to arise. This excruciating doubt about the authenticity of his mission was the means God used to heal his overidentification with the role of ascetic. Any overidentification hinders our acceptance of God as God is. The God of pure faith keeps interfering with our ideas about who God is. Jesus' response to the question raised by John's disciples was to work the kinds of miracles that Isaiah had foretold the Messiah would work, thus reassuring John with actions rather than words: "You were not mistaken; I am the Messiah."

Jesus said to his disciples, "Who is my mother?" The answer is: those who do the will of God, not just those who think about doing it. The spiritual journey is the letting go of roles, not the fulfillment of them. If we lose our role, we don't lose ourselves; we just think we do. In place of our idea of ourselves, God gives us himself.

7

A NONJUDGMENTAL ATTITUDE

Then each went to his own house, while Jesus went to the Mount of Olives. But early in the morning he arrived again in the Temple area, and all the people started coming to him, and he sat down and taught them. Then the scribes and the Pharisees brought a woman who had been caught in adultery and made her stand in the middle. They said to him, "Teacher, this woman was caught in the very act of committing adultery. Now in the law, Moses commanded us to stone such women. So what do you say?" They said this to test him, so that they could have some charge to bring against him. Jesus bent down and began to write on the ground with his finger. But when they continued asking him, he straightened up and said to them, "Let the one among you who is without sin be the first to throw a stone at her." Again he bent down and wrote on the ground. And in response, they went away one by one, beginning with the elders. So he was left alone with the woman before him. Then Jesus straightened up and said to her, "Woman, where are they? Has no one condemned you?" She replied, "No one, sir." Then Jesus said, "Neither do I condemn you. Go [and] from now on do not sin any more."

(John 8:1–11)

Jesus' enemies were not interested in this unfortunate woman; she just happened to serve their purposes. Her sin provided them with what seemed like the perfect trap in which to catch Jesus.

Whichever way he answered their carefully prepared question, they were sure he would be in trouble. If he said, "Yes, stone her," he would be going against the compassionate teaching he had been giving. If he said, "Don't stone her," they could say that he was not upholding the Law of Moses. He could then be brought before the authorities and accused of denigrating the Law. They thought they had Jesus all wrapped up.

So they dragged the woman in front of him as he was teaching in the Temple precincts and said, "This woman has been caught in the act of adultery. The Law of Moses has ordered such women to be stoned. What is your opinion?" Their hypocrisy was clear. Not only were they representing themselves as righteous observers of the Law, but they were using the observance of the Law as an excuse to bring about Jesus' destruction.

The people hanging on Jesus' words were shocked and waited with bated breath to hear what he would answer. But he said nothing. Instead he bent down and started writing with his finger in the sand. What did this gesture mean? We read that God wrote the Ten Commandments with his finger on stone tablets. Perhaps Jesus was subtly affirming his divine authority as he wrote with his finger in the sand.

A more down-to-earth interpretation also comes to mind. There used to be a practice called doodling. Doodling is what you do when you are listening absent-mindedly to a lecture. Maybe this is what Jesus was doing. It was a nonverbal communication meaning, "I'm bored!"

The accusers of the woman were not about to let him out of the trap. So they kept pressing him, "What are we to do, Master? What is your solution to this case?"

When they persisted, Jesus straightened up and said, "Let the person who has no sin be the first to cast a stone at her." Thus, he did not deny them the right to carry out this prescription of the Law, but he insisted on one condition, namely, that they have no sin on their consciences. Then he bent down and continued doodling.

The crowd began to thin out. The elders were the first to recognize that they could not throw any stones under the condition that Jesus had imposed. The younger zealots of the Law were the last to go. At last, Jesus and the woman were left alone.

Jesus looked up and said, "Woman, where are they?" Notice the irony of the question: "Has no one condemned you?" Evidently, the self-righteous observers of the Law, so eager to throw stones, could not measure up to the requirement that Jesus had laid down.

The woman answered, "No one." Jesus said, "Neither do I condemn you."

Here, as in the parables, Jesus challenges the value system of his hearers: "What is your motive for this action? Are you ready to take responsibility for it?"

By refusing to judge the woman, Jesus identifies with her. He does not preach to her. He shows his love by refusing to judge her, thus allowing her to judge herself. On other occasions, Jesus ate and drank with public sinners. Sharing a meal was the sign of belonging to a group, family, or nation. Jesus thus chose to belong to the company of sinners — not by sharing in their sins, of course, but by sharing the social consequences of their sins.

Jesus also showed love to the people who were accusing her. The statement, "Let the one among you who has no sin be the first to cast a stone at her," was not meant merely to contravene their trap. It was an invitation to the accusers to look into their own consciences and to recognize that they, too, were sinners. We are reminded of the divine compassion revealed in the parable of the prodigal son. We first hear of God's mercy toward the prodigal son's obvious misbehavior. Then we learn of God's mercy toward his self-righteous brother who turned out to be a sinner too, only he was not aware of it; hence, he was more difficult to help.

Jesus' passion and death are his ultimate identification with sinners. Just as he identified with the woman and her accusers, so he also identifies with us and the suffering that is the consequence of our sins.

8

REPENTANCE AS REORIENTATION

A Pharisee invited him to dine with him, and he entered the
Pharisee's house and reclined at table. Now there was a sinful
woman in the city who learned that he was at table in the house
of the Pharisee. Bringing an alabaster flask of ointment, she stood
behind him at his feet weeping and began to bathe his feet with
her tears. Then she wiped them with her hair, kissed them, and
anointed them with the ointment. When the Pharisee who had
invited him saw this, he said to himself, "If this man were a
prophet, he would know who and what sort of woman this is who
is touching him, that she is a sinner." Jesus said to him in reply,
"Simon, I have something to say to you." "Tell me, teacher," he
said. "Two people were in debt to a certain creditor; one owed five
hundred days' wages and the other owed fifty. Since they were
unable to repay the debt, he forgave it for both. Which of them will
love him more?" Simon said in reply, "The one, I suppose, whose
larger debt was forgiven." He said to him, "You have judged
rightly." Then he turned to the woman and said to Simon, "Do
you see this woman? When I entered your house, you did not give
me water for my feet, but she has bathed them with her tears and
wiped them with her hair. You did not give me a kiss, but she has
not ceased kissing my feet since the time I entered. You did not
anoint my head with oil, but she anointed my feet with ointment.
So I tell you, her many sins have been forgiven; hence, she has
shown great love. But the one to whom little is forgiven, loves

little." He said to her, "Your sins are forgiven." The others at table
said to themselves, "Who is this who even forgives sins?" But he
said to the woman, "Your faith has saved you; go in peace."
(Luke 7:36–50)

To understand this story, it is important to remember that in
this society a distinguished guest was normally offered three signs
of welcome. Water was provided to wash his feet, his head was
anointed with oil, and he was given a kiss. Jesus was invited to the
pharisee's house but was not offered any of these courtesies. Since
Jesus was a distinguished rabbi, preacher, and healer, to have these
normal courtesies withheld was an insult. The omission was not
lost upon this woman who was a sinner in the neighborhood. What
was not known was that she had ceased to be a sinner. As soon
as we change our basic orientation, that is the end of our former
worldview and whatever we were along with it. Similarly, every
time we move to a new level of faith, all our previous relationships
are reshaped. The Book of Revelation quotes God as saying, "Behold, I make everything new." God loves to make everything new,
especially people. This woman was no longer a sinner because she
had repented. God is present only in the present and responds to
where we are in the present.

The guests noticed the pharisee's treatment. They realized that
he had invited Jesus to the house to look him over — to check him
out. Jesus graciously acquiesced. Jesus plays along with all kinds of
mixed motivations, not to mention bad ones, using them as points
of departure to improve the situation.

This woman was appalled that he had not received the normal courtesies. She decided to provide them in her own way. She
rained tears on his feet and wiped them with her hair. She poured
perfumes over his feet and kissed them. Thus, she pushed all the
ordinary courtesies beyond the ordinary. This might have caused
the pharisee to withhold judgment, or turn it on himself, but instead his superego activated and he reflected, "For such a woman
to touch a rabbi in public is unheard of! If this man were a prophet,
he would know what kind of woman this is and not permit such
service."

Jesus, knowing his thoughts, said to him, " What would you say if two people owed two debts — one enormous and the other modest — and the creditor forgave them both? Which of the two would be more grateful?"

"The one who owed the greater," Simon answered.

Jesus then proceeds to point out the courtesies that Simon had withheld. He compares Simon's treatment to that of the woman. "I came to your house and you didn't give me water for my feet. She, instead of water, has provided tears. You gave me no kiss, but she has not ceased kissing my feet since I came in. You did not anoint my head with oil, but she anointed my feet with perfume. I tell you her many sins are forgiven because of her great love. To one who shows little love, little has been forgiven." This final statement implies that the pharisee is still in his sins.

Then Jesus says to her, "Your sins are forgiven." Why? Because she manifested such great love — the sign that she had been forgiven. Great love has to be manifested.

Jesus says to her, "Your faith has saved you." Faith in what? Faith in his infinite mercy. That is the source of forgiveness: not good deeds, religious observances, austerities, but faith in the infinite mercy of God. Faith is opening and surrendering to God. Faith grows by maintaining that openness in spite of trials, affliction, and failure. The formula for ultimate transformation is boundless confidence in divine love.

9

THE BIRTH OF SPIRITUAL ATTENTIVENESS

Now as they went on their way, he entered a village; and a woman named Martha received him into her house. And she had a sister called Mary who sat at the Lord's feet and listened to his teaching. But Martha was distracted with much serving; and she went to him and said, "Lord, do you not care that my sister has left me to serve alone? Tell her to help me." But the Lord answered her, "Martha, Martha, you are anxious and troubled about many things; one thing is needful. Mary has chosen the good portion, which shall not be taken away from her." (Luke 10:38–42)

Mary of Bethany sitting at the feet of Jesus and listening to his discourse is a paradigm of the first stirrings of contemplation. As she sat listening to his words, a kind of blurring of the conceptual level took place that carried her far beyond Martha's busy world of tasks and obligations. This blurring was the result of her attraction to go beyond words to the Word — beyond the details of his humanity to the person who was speaking — and to enter into union with that person.

Mary of Bethany models how a developing relationship with Christ moves beyond mere acquaintanceship with his words and teachings to an actual communion with his being. To commune is to rest in the gift of each other's presence without feeling one has to say or do something. The gift of oneself to God and of God

42

to us is exactly what contemplation, understood in its traditional meaning, is.

From the perspective of our own developing friendship with Christ, the words of scripture are conversation pieces leading to communion. *Lectio divina* is the oldest method of Christian meditation. Literally, *lectio divina* means reading — or more precisely, *listening* — to the text we believe to be divinely inspired. The practice of *lectio divina* is not designed to learn something on the conceptual level. Still less is it a study of the Bible, which is useful at another time. It is the reading of scripture with utmost reverence as an encounter with Christ. Through reflection on the sacred texts, one's imagination, memory, and reasoning are habituated to the mind of Christ and to his way of thinking and feeling. One's understanding of the Gospel and one's response to it are simplified to a single aspiration or even to a single word. This leads beyond conversation to moments of communing with God.

As we listen to the words of scripture during our time of *lectio divina*, reflect on various aspects of a particular text, and respond with gratitude, humility, love, sorrow, joy, or other emotions, we may feel, like Mary, a blurring of the conceptual level. As we interiorize the content of the message, Jesus becomes not just a concept, but a person; not a picture or statue, but a living presence. The regular practice of *lectio divina* awakens the Christ who is asleep within us. This awakening might be called the birth of spiritual attentiveness. The purpose of every spiritual discipline, ritual, sacrament, and text of scripture is to awaken the divine presence that is already there.

Once spiritual attentiveness has been awakened in us, it can be nurtured and deepened during times of prayer by specific contemplative practices. To maintain that attentiveness, one may use a short phrase or word to sustain the general, loving awareness of God's presence. The prayer phrase or word — it could be "God," "Abba," "Peace," "Come, Lord," etc. — symbolizes our intention to consent to the divine presence and action within us. We become aware of the general loving presence of God beyond concepts, feelings, and particular acts. A "cloud of unknowing" is woven by repeated practice in letting go of our thoughts and preoccupations and consenting to the divine presence. In time, it becomes a habit by means of which we can move into that presence almost at will. By not knowing in the way we usually know, the knowledge of God through love manifests itself in our prayer. The gentle activity of consenting to God during the time of contemplative prayer sustains spiritual attentiveness and distinguishes it from mere emptiness of mind. It is rather, the emptiness of self. The divine presence fills that emptiness and transforms our motivation into that of the Spirit.

One who is visually oriented may prefer an inward gaze upon God during prayer. In this practice it is not only we who are looking at God, but God is looking at us. If we are enveloped by the loving gaze of God, we do not have to do anything to obtain God's attention. Our proper response is to consent and to surrender.

A third method of sustaining spiritual attentiveness is based on the breath. This practice consists of identifying our normal breathing with inhaling the divine Spirit and exhaling divine love into the universe. Once these methods of interiorization have awakened spiritual attentiveness, we habitually rest in the presence of the Mystery beyond words and particular acts, except to maintain the intention of loving, reverent, waiting upon God in pure faith.

The general loving presence of God in pure faith is accessed by the discrete use of each of these three sacred symbols: listening to the word of God, gazing upon God, or breathing the Spirit. As we move into interior silence and feel called to rest in God, it is *as if* we were listening, *as if* we were seeing, *as if* we were breathing. But we do not hear any word; we do not see any image; we do not feel any breath. The spiritual senses are analogies. As spiritual attentiveness is awakened by these sacred symbols, the symbols themselves are left behind and the Spirit invites us into union with the Reality to which the symbols point. Beyond the spiritual senses, the conviction of God's abiding presence and action within crowns the process of divine transformation.

10

AWAKENING THE SPIRITUAL SENSES

Now there was a man full of leprosy in one of the towns where he was; and when he saw Jesus, he fell prostrate, pleaded with him, and said, "Lord, if you wish, you can make me clean." Jesus stretched out his hand, touched him, and said, "I do will it. Be made clean." And the leprosy left him immediately. Then he ordered him not to tell anyone, but "Go, show yourself to the priest and offer for your cleansing what Moses prescribed; that will be proof for them." The report about him spread all the more, and great crowds assembled to listen to him and to be cured of their ailments, but he would withdraw to deserted places to pray.

(Luke 5:12–17)

Jesus reached out and touched the leper and his infirmity immediately departed. On the visible plane, Jesus cured the leper as reported in Luke. The meaning of scripture, however, extends beyond the visible to the invisible reality of God's power, which aims at the healing of the whole person. Thus, we can say that the miracles of Jesus are not mere bodily healings, but are designed to awaken the spiritual senses.

The sacraments of Eucharist, Baptism, and Confirmation are movements in which Jesus provides the same graces that he provided in his own time when he reached out and touched physical wounds. By his touch, he enlivens the spiritual senses.

There are three stages of inner healing and liberation from the roots of sin, which the Fathers of the Church called the spiritual senses. The spiritual sense of smell is the first grace; the spiritual sense of touch is a more profound grace; the greatest grace is the spiritual sense of taste. These spiritual experiences represent, respectively, the attraction, the proximity, and the communication of the divine presence.

The birth of spiritual attentiveness — face-to-face, being-to-being communing with Christ — is presented by the Fathers as the spiritual sense of smell. Smell is the attraction or aversion that one experiences when a delightful or disagreeable odor is in the neighborhood. It does not take long for the olfactory apparatus to say yes or no to a particular scent. If it is wisteria or perfume, we are charmed; if it is garlic or something unpleasant, we move to another room.

The spiritual sense of smell is manifested by the inner attraction for prayer, solitude, and silence — to be still and to wait upon God with loving attentiveness. The attraction draws us irresistibly to our encounter with Christ even when he does not seem to show up for long periods. The words of the Canticle, "Your name spoken is a spreading perfume.... Draw me! We will follow you eagerly!" (Song 2:3–4) do not mean that we experience the scent of delicious perfume. Rather, we experience the inner attraction of God *as if* the divine presence was a delicious odor arising from within and attracting us to itself.

The spiritual sense of touch is a further development of spiritual attentiveness. John resting in the bosom of Jesus at the Last Supper is a lively image of this grace. The word for "bosom" signifies that he was resting in the hollow of Jesus' chest; that is, in the valley between the breasts, suggesting that he could not get any closer to Jesus' heart. Listening to the heartbeat of the Savior, he was inwardly immersed in divine love. The spiritual sense of touch is the experience of being interiorly embraced by God. The Spirit, so to speak, plants a great big kiss in the middle of our spirit and breathes into our will, the mouth of the spirit, the breath of life. Our whole being experiences God not only as an attraction but as an immediate presence.

A still more profound divine communication is conveyed in the analogy of the sense of taste. The psalmist urges us to open to this grace in the words, "Taste and see that the Lord is sweet" (Ps.34:9). It is one thing to be close enough to touch another person or to be touched; it is something else to penetrate the inmost being of the other. Only God who dwells within can be experienced at such an intimate level.

When we consume food, we transform it into ourselves and it becomes part of our bodies. In divine union the presence of God arises not only as an irresistible attraction or embrace, but as a unifying presence in our inmost being. This is the grace of Pentecost: Christ living our life, or more exactly, living us.

Just as the perfume of the Beloved is transcended by the divine touch and the divine touch by the divine taste, there is an even greater grace than the transient experience of divine union. Beyond any experience, however spiritual and profound, there is the mystery of pure faith and pure love. God, the divine energy, is so powerful and so intimate that no human faculty can perceive the divine presence in its purity. But faith receives it by consenting. The growing conviction of faith, fruit of the purification of the unconscious, sees God in everything and everything in God.

The growth of faith and love frees us from our expectations and from attachment to the unfolding of the spiritual senses. Contemplation is manifested not only by the spiritual senses, the "felt" presence of God, and by the ever-deepening absorption of the faculties in God's presence. It is equally manifested through the conviction of pure faith, which believes that the divine Word is continuously addressed to our spirit but at a level that we cannot perceive in this life. This secret transmission is the essence of contemplation. John of the Cross calls it the hidden ladder leading to transforming union.

While this deepening of faith may be a gradual process, healing itself is not. The leper was instantly cured. Whatever the word of God says happens instantly. This indicates the sublimity of the touch; it was not just a pat on the back. It was the end of his disease. Similarly, when the inward touch takes place in contemplative prayer and Jesus commands, "Peace be with you," it does not matter whether you are in the biggest storm of your life; you are instantly at peace. When the dark night could not be darker and everything is going wrong, the Lord simply says, "Peace," or "Be still," or as he said to the leper, "Be cured," and peace is immediately experienced.

The universe came into being when God said, "Let there be light." In his miracles God says, "Let there be life!" Thus, in a deep period of stress or a prolonged absence of consolation, all of a sudden, Jesus touches our inmost being. Healing flows on every level and all our woes are forgotten as if they had never happened.

The touches of the Spirit are transforming. They point to a gradual change of consciousness. Transformation of consciousness into the mind of Christ is the goal of contemplative prayer.

THE PARABLES

11

INTENTIONALITY AND CONSENT

The kingdom of heaven is like a treasure buried in a field, which a person finds and hides again, and out of joy goes and sells all that he has and buys that field. Again, the kingdom of heaven is like a merchant searching for fine pearls. When he finds a pearl of great price, he goes and sells all that he has and buys it. Again, the kingdom of heaven is like a net thrown into the sea, which collects fish of every kind. When it is full they haul it ashore and sit down to put what is good into buckets. What is bad they throw away. Thus it will be at the end of the age. The angels will go out and separate the wicked from the righteous and throw them into the fiery furnace, where there will be wailing and grinding of teeth.

"Do you understand all these things?" They answered, "Yes." And he replied, "Then every scribe who has been instructed in the kingdom of heaven is like the head of a household who brings from his storeroom both the new and the old." When Jesus finished these parables, he went away from there. (Matthew 13:44–54)

The parables in this series, each in its own way, reflect a certain light on the reign of God. The first parable is about one who discovered buried treasure in a field. At the time of the Gospel, this was not unusual. In days gone by, people used to bury their treasures to protect them. This man was lucky enough to hit a treasure chest while plowing a field. He went and bought the field.

51

Another man was looking for fine pearls, and when he found one, he sold everything and bought that pearl. The reign of God is the pearl of great price or the treasure hidden in the field. The reign of God is the discovery of the divine presence and action within us. The reign of God is happiness. If you find the reign of God, you don't need anything else; it relativizes all other treasures. It is the focusing of one's value system. Jesus describes this focusing in another parable as a single eye. It is the purity of intention that arises not by our efforts but by the discovery of the divine presence within. This is the gift, but it does not take effect until we awaken to its presence and submit to its action.

The key to happiness is the presence of God as a growing conviction, as a presence that integrates and penetrates all our activity, transforming every human faculty and potentiality. The true Self is the divine presence within us working through our particular uniqueness. Intentionality, then, is basically the orientation to the treasure within us, to the pearl of great price, which is the awareness of the divine presence and action within.

This is the focus of the centering prayer practice. We do not constantly recreate our intention. In these parables, these people didn't keep digging for treasure or keep buying the same pearl again and again. They committed themselves once and for all because of the value they saw in their discoveries. Once we have chosen the reign of God and decided to pursue it, it becomes the basic source out of which all our actions emerge, the good soil in which the divine seed grows.

Intentionality connects to the divine energy within us. In centering prayer we immerse ourselves in our commitment to Christ, in our original intention of buying the pearl and of plugging into the reign of God. It is not so much we who initiate; rather, we consent to God's presence and action within us. We consent to God's intentionality. As Paul says, "In love he destined us for adoption to himself through Jesus Christ, in accord with the favor of his will" (Eph. 1:5). So the intention that enables us to enter the reign of God is not a bright idea of our own. It is rather submission to the divine intentionality that is calling us into the kingdom.

The more focused our intention, the more powerful it is. Our intention is submission to God's intention. We are not the generators of our good works or of our relationship with God. We perceive, rather, that we are receivers of the divine life, which does not belong to us, but which is entrusted to us if we consent.

We come now to the parable of the net thrown into the sea that pulled in all kinds of fish. Notice that it was not pulled in until it was filled. This is a revelation of how the reign of God works; it does not come to us prepackaged with our name on it. It evolves. The human condition is like the net full of fish and various kinds of junk that have been thrown into the sea. The junk is precisely what the Spirit separates out in the dark nights. The Spirit puts the good stuff into containers and throws out the rest. The Spirit works through our personal history layer by layer, preserving the values of each stage and throwing out what is worthless. This separation does not occur until the Spirit has moved us to the decisive moment of harvesting, which takes place when the Spirit's work of purifying our unconscious has reached a certain completion. Then we can say with St. John of the Cross, "My one activity is love." What other ministry is there? Whatever else we do, unless it comes from that intentionality, is more or less ineffective.

The Cloud of Unknowing makes a distinction between acts of will and love. Love is the abiding intentionality out of which particular acts of will emerge. In this situation, whatever one does has the effectiveness of apostolic love, a term that the early monastic fathers used to refer to the love the apostles experienced when the Holy Spirit took possession of them at Pentecost. That is the source of every true apostolate.

12

DISCERNMENT

The kingdom of heaven is like a treasure buried in a field, which a person finds and hides again, and out of joy goes and sells all that he has and buys that field. Again, the kingdom of heaven is like a merchant searching for fine pearls. When he finds a pearl of great price, he goes and sells all that he has and buys it. Again, the kingdom of heaven is like a net thrown into the sea, which collects fish of every kind. When it is full they haul it ashore and sit down to put what is good into buckets. What is bad they throw away. Thus it will be at the end of the age. The angels will go out and separate the wicked from the righteous and throw them into the fiery furnace, where there will be wailing and grinding of teeth.

"Do you understand all these things?" They answered, "Yes." And he replied, "Then every scribe who has been instructed in the kingdom of heaven is like the head of a household who brings from his storeroom both the new and the old." When Jesus finished these parables, he went away from there. (Matthew 13:44–54)

As Jesus concluded these arresting parables, he asked the crowd with a great sense of irony, "Do you understand?" They said, "Yes!" He then said: "Every scribe learned in the reign of God knows how to bring forth out of his treasures new things and old." Some people can bring out all kinds of new things, but very little out of tradition. And some people can bring out the old stuff ad nauseam.

Neither are teachers that Jesus considers apt for the reign of God. Fidelity to the old and openness to the new were magnificently represented by Pope John XXIII. The signs of the times that he recommended to the consideration of the bishops at the Vatican Council are a revelation of God just as much as things long since past. The living tradition alone passes on the full Christian life. The church constantly has to integrate new wisdom, new science, new information into the Gospel if she is going to communicate it to contemporary people and to people of other cultures. Unfortunately, those of little faith tend to identify the values of the Gospel with particular structures or symbols. Then if the symbol is modified, like turning the altar around or receiving communion in the hand, they think the values of the Gospel are being rejected. People have to grow beyond this overidentification. Ancient symbols can sometimes prevent the value of the Gospel from being fully transmitted in new circumstances. Even words develop opposite meanings over time. Would we say that Jesus was not in continuity with Moses and the prophets? They bore witness to him on the mountain. Yet he was completely free about following their tradition. He paid no attention to the rabbinical practices of preaching only in synagogues and only with regard to scripture.

It is precisely the intentionality of love that goes beyond human rules, customs, and mindsets and enables the church to present the message of the Gospel in the way that it can best be heard in particular circumstances of time and place. When this hasn't been done, as we read again and again in history, the moment of grace is lost to the church. In China, the Jesuit Father Matteo Ricci intuited the way to present the Gospel to the Buddhists. He was accepted by the people. His influence was growing. But one of the other orders couldn't bear to see a Jesuit missionary succeeding. History gives us the mournful news that they succeeded in obtaining from the Roman authorities the suppression of the mission. So Ricci came home and so did the Gospel. If he had been allowed to continue, who knows what the later history of China might have been? He was ahead of his time. Maybe we should say that certain people in the church were behind the times. Or as Pope John XXIII would have said, they could not read the signs of the times. Jesus expects us to discern how the Gospel is to be transmitted once we have absorbed and assimilated it through *lectio divina*, prayer, and the service of community.

The reign of God involves a social dimension, not just the sifting of our own motivation. It involves the ability to sift the wheat from the chaff. Many religious communities today are trying to recover their charism and to discern what they were sent by the Spirit to do, and not just keep doing what they happen to be doing because of historical conditions. Jesus recommends this discernment for the building up of his body the church, to which we have a responsibility to share whatever we have been given.

13

"WHERE ARE YOU?"

On that day, Jesus went out of the house and sat down by the sea.
Such large crowds gathered around him that he got into a boat
and sat down, and the whole crowd stood along the shore. And he
spoke to them at length in parables, saying: "A sower went out to
sow. And as he sowed, some seed fell on the path and birds came
and ate it up. Some fell on rocky ground, where it had little soil.
It sprang up at once because the soil was not deep, and when the
sun rose it was scorched, and it withered for lack of roots. Some
seed fell among thorns, and the thorns grew up and choked it.
But some seed fell on rich soil, and produced fruit, a hundred or
sixty or thirtyfold. Whoever has ears ought to hear."

(Matthew 13:1–9)

In the parable of the sower Jesus seems to be referring to his
own preaching. Some of the seed, he says, falls on the footpath,
that is, on the hardpan, the path that goes through the field but
that has no give, no flexibility, and is almost as hard as concrete. To
translate that into modern terms, the word of God sometimes falls
on the sidewalks of New York or Amarillo, to mention only two
great cities. There is no chance of this seed bearing fruit because it
can't get through the concrete. The concrete represents the mythic
membership level of consciousness and the worldviews in which
people live with unquestioning presuppositions and preconceived
ideas: the world of racism, sexism, prejudice, and every kind of bias.

We have to take for granted that we bring to our listening to the word of God a certain amount of hardpan in our consciousness, made up of the unquestioned values and assumptions of parents, peer groups, and teachers that we absorbed in early childhood, especially during the socialization period from four to ten. All of these powerful influences have programmed our understanding of reality.

The parables are earthquakes shaking the ground from under our presuppositions and prepackaged values in order that a few cracks in the sidewalk might appear, enabling some of the seed to fall in between the cracks and produce at least a few weeds. The upsetting of our preconceived ideas is not a disaster; it is a necessity in order to hear the word of God. Thus, trials that upset our preconceived values are a great gift from God. Notice the succinctness of this one sentence: "Some seed fell upon the footpath." It addresses one obstacle to the hearing of the word of God as it is sown and not according to our interpretation. The interpretation is often not our own, but one we have absorbed from other people, our culture, ethnic group, and early religious training.

Let's look at the fate of the other seed. "Some fell on rocky ground." New England farms bring forth a new crop of rocks every spring no matter how many one picks up the previous year. That's why you have rock walls everywhere in New England. Although the word of God may be received with a certain openness, there is no substance to rocky soil. The seed when it grows up can't withstand the wind, the heat, and the rain. Perhaps this image points to those rocks in us that are compulsive activity or habits that resist change.

Some seeds fell on fertile soil, but there were already other things there, namely thorns, thistles, and weeds. When the word of God started to grow, it was choked by the lure of money, power, and pleasure-seeking.

Finally, some seed fell on good soil: not much in the way of weeds or briars, with depth to it and a looseness into which the seed could sink its roots. The soil suggests receptivity. The other soils were receptive too, but because of their varying forms of resistance, the word could not get through.

The parables are not moralistic. They are earth-shattering. They break up our prepackaged values and preconceived ideas and thus raise the fundamental question addressed to Adam and Eve after the Fall: "Where are you?"

The answer is we are in one of those four categories. We are confronted by reality in the parables in a way that forces us to enter into ourselves and to ask the right questions. We want to do good and we don't. We don't want to do bad and we do. That's the situation. The only answer is to turn over our unmanageable lives to the Higher Power.

When we come to contemplative prayer we are talking about the divine seed in its most pure form. The word of God is addressing now with a certain vigor each of those areas in us that resemble the different kinds of soil that Jesus differentiates in the parable. The divine light attacks whatever is resistant in us. There is something in us that does not quite want to let go. We want to hear, but just so much. We want to loosen up our hardpan, but not yet! Yes, we are open, except for... We want to give in, but do we? And so the great question, "Where are you?" arises with great urgency. Hanging on? Resisting? Loving the old presuppositions that seem to provide some security? Or still locked into the emotional programs for happiness?

Since we won't let go in some areas, the Divine Therapist keeps bringing up the same old issues. Relentlessly. Tenderly but firmly; consoling but also tough at times. The pain of realizing that something has to go that we love, are attached to, and depend on keeps gnawing away.

How much do we want to hear the word of God? That is the question. "Will this ultimate confrontation wipe me out? Will my self, that dear thing that I love so much — that causes me nothing but pain, but still the only self I know — have to go? Where will I be? Where will I go?"

"Where are you?"

14

PERSEVERANCE IN PRAYER

Then he told them a parable about the necessity for them to pray always without becoming weary. He said, "There was a judge in a certain town who neither feared God nor respected any human being. And a widow in that town used to come to him and say, 'Render a just decision for me against my adversary.' For a long time the judge was unwilling, but eventually he thought, 'While it is true that I neither fear God nor respect any human being, because this widow keeps bothering me I shall deliver a just decision for her lest she finally come and strike me.'" The Lord said, "Pay attention to what the dishonest judge says. Will not God then secure the rights of his chosen ones who call out to him day and night? Will he be slow to answer them? I tell you, he will see to it that justice is done for them speedily. But when the Son of Man comes, will he find faith on earth?" (Luke 18:1–8)

The purpose of this parable is to encourage us to pray continuously and not to lose heart, to keep asking for what we need. It is a far-out tale with a certain humor about it that is characteristic of the parables. The widow is a symbol of everyone in some kind of need. She evidently was being pursued by her insurance company. She was pounding on the door of this judge saying, "Help, help, help! I need this money and this company is after it. Do me justice."

The judge couldn't care less about justice, God, or this lady's plight. He was only interested in himself. She finally wore him out by pounding on his door, calling him on the phone, sending him telegrams. Finally he said, "I can't put up with this anymore. I'll let her win the case because I'm fed up with being pursued day and night by her persistence." That is a humorous way of presenting the goodness of God. We don't often think of God that way. If we just badger God enough, God will respond. So gimme, gimme, gimme has a certain power according to this text. Jesus says, "Don't give up. If this unjust judge finally caved in, will not God in his goodness provide the help that you need if you keep asking?"

Why doesn't God answer us more promptly? Why do we have to wait so long and why don't we get more of the things that we ask for?

There is another place in scripture in which Jesus seems to take the role of a severe judge. That is the situation in which the Canaanite woman came asking for the cure of her daughter. Since Jesus had provided all kinds of miraculous cures, she didn't expect to meet with any hesitation. He didn't respond to her at all, even when the apostles interceded on her behalf. He didn't reply when she prostrated herself with her nose in the dust and pleaded. When she persisted, he insulted her saying that it was not possible to give the food of the children to dogs. She received from him silence, insult, and rejection; yet she kept waiting, hoping, and asking. At last she said, "I'm not asking for much, just a few crumbs. Forget about the bread." This is the faith that finally cracked the armor of God. Jesus exclaimed, "Your faith is great indeed! You can have anything you want!"

Notice it was only after silence, insult, rejection, and the apparent failure of her prayer that Jesus acted. This delay is not an infrequent experience of sincere seekers of God when they have what seems to them to be a very important need. The Canaanite woman just kept hanging on. Notice that her physical position moved from standing to kneeling to prostrating, a symbol perhaps that this silence of God was doing an enormous amount of constructive work by increasing her faith and bringing it to the one-pointedness that pierced through every obstacle and touched the heart of God.

Silence is one answer to prayer. God responds not so much by granting individual requests but by changing us from inside. Prayer is not designed to change God or the situation, but to change us. If the external circumstances are helpful to that end, we may receive our request. If there is a possibility that our faith will grow in this mysterious dialogue between our petitions and the divine silence, we may not have our request granted. In other words, prayer is designed to increase faith, which is not a particular petition for anything, but the total surrender of ourselves to God. Faith means entrusting the whole of ourselves to the infinite mercy of God. It is a continual prayer. The particular favors that concern us often belong to an immature level of faith. The dialogue between the Canaanite woman and Jesus is also our experience of prayer over a number of years, perhaps twenty or thirty, in which as a result of persevering, God brings us to the fundamental attitude of prayer that is not a particular petition, but an attitude of total receptivity to the primary message of the universe, which is love. That message produces the kingdom both in us and outside. The reign of God isn't just in us; it is also everywhere else. By accessing it in ourselves, we can perceive it everywhere else.

Faith dissolves the enormous illusion of the human condition, which is that God is absent. This great lie, the source of all human misery, prevents the free flow of the divine life and love into us and into the world. The purpose of continuous prayer is to access that which is most true about us, namely, our divine Source. The divine is always manifesting itself, though mostly in secret, to those who walk in the presence of God and allow this presence to influence all their relationships.

CELEBRATIONS
OF JESUS' PRESENCE

15

LONGING FOR THE LIGHT

"Be watchful! Be alert! You do not know when the time will come. It is like a man traveling abroad. He leaves home and places his servants in charge, each with his work, and orders the gatekeeper to be on the watch. Watch, therefore; you do not know when the lord of the house is coming, whether in the evening, or at midnight, or at cockcrow, or in the morning. May he not come suddenly and find you sleeping. What I say to you, I say to all: 'Watch!' " (Mark 13:33–37)

The first Sunday of Advent addresses the theological theme of divine light, which the liturgy investigates in great depth during this season. Today with our newfound discoveries in quantum mechanics and physics, we know that light is a form of energy. This energy is invisible to the naked eye and elusive to the most sophisticated kinds of receptive apparatus. This marvelous sun of ours is just a shadow compared to the divine light, a flicker of a dying flame enabling us to see with our bodily eyes. Faith is the receptive apparatus that perceives the divine energy. Advent is a refining of our receptive apparatus. One of the best ways of doing this is to watch and pray.

Three major figures in Advent symbolize the basic attitudes that are involved in waiting and watching. One of these is Isaiah. Listen to the longing of Isaiah: "Oh, that you would rend the heavens and come down!"(Isa. 64:19)

The spirit of Advent is the realization that we cannot be happy without a relationship with this immense Mystery that vastly transcends all categories and yet deals with us in an incredibly personal way. The grace of Advent, through the Spirit's gift of Knowledge, penetrates the inadequacy of all appearances. In Advent we perceive our misguided and distorted values and programs for happiness. We know that we cannot save ourselves. Hence, out of our inmost being comes the cry for help. The realization comes that there is nothing we can do to change the existential situation except to wait and to offer this longing, too deep for words, to God's infinite compassion.

The second figure of Advent is John the Baptist. His first words to his disciples are "Repent!" which means "change the direction in which you are looking for happiness." He was inviting the people of his time to enter into the Advent mystery by letting go of the obstacles to divine life, light, and love — the ingredients without which we cannot be happy.

The third figure of Advent is Mary, the Virgin Mother of the Savior. Her presence in the Advent liturgy makes our anguish comprehensible; otherwise, it would be existential dread. The feeling of anguish is mitigated by the sure hope of God's coming to those who are waiting. It may be delayed — evening, midnight, cockcrow, dawn, in the morning — but the coming is certain.

Mary symbolizes God's coming into our hearts with his transforming presence. Longing for the light eventually brings the light. Faith opens into trust, and trust is not disappointed because the love of God is poured forth in the hearts of the brokenhearted. Our hearts have to be broken in the sense of realizing that our projects for happiness cannot possibly work. Our longing to be whole can come about only by God's gift; all we can do is wait for it. To know how to wait for God is the greatest of all knowledge. Out of that knowledge comes the cry that pierces the heavens. Advent is not just waiting for a feast. It is waiting for God, waiting to be reborn, waiting to be transformed.

16

OPENING TO THE GIFT

In the sixth month, the angel Gabriel was sent from God to a town of Galilee called Nazareth, to a virgin betrothed to a man named Joseph, of the house of David, and the virgin's name was Mary. And coming to her, he said, "Hail, favored one! The Lord is with you." But she was greatly troubled at what was said and pondered what sort of greeting this might be. Then the angel said to her, "Do not be afraid, Mary, for you have found favor with God. Behold, you will conceive in your womb and bear a son, and you shall name him Jesus. He will be great and will be called Son of the Most High, and the Lord God will give him the throne of David his father, and he will rule over the house of Jacob forever, and of his kingdom there will be no end."

But Mary said to the angel, "How can this be, since I have no relations with a man?"

And the angel said to her in reply, "The holy Spirit will come upon you, and the power of the Most High will overshadow you. Therefore the child to be born will be called holy, the Son of God. And behold, Elizabeth, your relative, has also conceived a son in her old age, and this is the sixth month for her who was called barren; for nothing will be impossible for God."

Mary said, "Behold, I am the handmaid of the Lord. May it be done to me according to your word." Then the angel departed from her. (Luke 1:26–38)

At this time of the year, children are extremely open to gifts. There is a special quality to their expectations that warms the heart. It is this childlike expectancy that we need to bring to the liturgy. The Christmas presents that we share are reminders of the incredible gifts of God. In receiving a Christmas gift, we are not just receiving a gift from a dear friend. It is a symbol of God's love for us, which is poured out with extraordinary largesse.

It is important to realize how the liturgy works. The lessons that are read on the great feasts of the year are not so much instruction as demonstrations of grace. The liturgy loves to express the effects of participation in the mystery of Christ through events in the Old and New Testaments that typify the gifts that we are now receiving in the celebration of particular feasts. The celebration thus becomes a parable of the particular aspect of the divine light and life that is being transmitted.

Here is an example: The common denominator of sacred history is the grace of Christ. In the Old Testament, this grace was offered in the form of types of what was to come. In the New Testament, the fulfillment of these types in the person of Jesus is laid out. The same grace is now present in the Christian community in all its fullness. This fullness is divided up throughout the liturgical year so that we are not overwhelmed by its extraordinary communication but can absorb it little by little. We don't eat just one enormous meal once a week, but eat a certain amount every day so that we can assimilate our needed nourishment bit by bit. Similarly, the liturgical year provides for the gradual assimilation of the mystery. Our faith is increased by the divine communication in dosages that we can enjoy. The sacred meals in the Old Testament symbolized belonging to God's people.

The liturgy is meant to be experiential. Everything we read about in the Old and New Testament and all that it symbolized in belonging to God's people and sharing in the divine life is bestowed, not just as information, but as experience. If we stop at mere instruction, we have missed the main event. The lessons and symbols reveal the graces that are being offered for the healing and enhancement of every level of our being.

The kind of openness that we bring to the liturgy is the key to understanding the Christmas/Epiphany mystery and to receiving it. The message is: We belong to the universe and to the God who created it. We belong to the God who is within us. We belong to the human family in which God dwells and manifests. The light and life of God are available in the measure of our increasing receptivity. Each year that we celebrate this opening to the gifts of God, we open more.

In today's Gospel event we hear how Mary's expectation of her vocation was shattered in an instant by the visit of an angel. This warns us that the shattering of our vision of life — the disappointments, the heartbreaks, rejection, loneliness, confusion — these things are part of the preparation for a greater vocation. Our personal history becomes sacred history. God never takes anything away without giving us something better. Sacred history is about how God prepared his people in order to give them the fullness of grace in Christ. Now that this fullness has come, our responsibility is to unpackage the incredible graces that the human family has received and of which we are now the stewards. If we come to the Christmas graces with this open heart and open mind, the grace of Christ is transmitted to us personally, enabling us to experience what the liturgy calls "the gifts of Christmas." Just listen to a few of them: divine adoption as children of God, anticipation of eternal joy, peace, conformity to Christ, participation in the divine life, understanding of the divine mysteries. This is the transmission of divine life. The trials of life are not obstacles to receiving it, but part of the reception. Even the greatest tragedies contain the triumph of God over suffering. As we pray for the gifts of Christmas, we realize that these words point to the life of Christ welling up within us and giving us the strength to make all our activity an act of divine love. "My one activity is love" (John of the Cross). The divine life within us is teaching us not only how to receive but how to give.

17

"SO TINY, SO IMMENSE..."

Now there were shepherds in that region living in the fields and
keeping the night watch over their flock. The angel of the Lord
appeared to them and the glory of the Lord shone around them,
and they were struck with great fear. The angel said to them, "Do
not be afraid; for behold, I proclaim to you good news of great
joy that will be for all the people. For today in the city of David
a savior has been born for you who is Messiah and Lord. And
this will be a sign for you: you will find an infant wrapped in
swaddling clothes and lying in a manger." And suddenly there
was a multitude of the heavenly host with the angel, praising
God and saying:
"Glory to God in the highest
and on earth peace to those on whom his favor rests."

(Luke 2:8–14)

The Christmas liturgy celebrates the three major comings of
Jesus: in the flesh, in our hearts, and at the Last Judgment. These
events are all interrelated. The Last Judgment is a future event that
the church, with her x-ray vision, looks at through the eyes of the
divine infant. He who made the light of the sun exploded into the
shepherds' world on this night, leaving them dazzled and terrified.
Yet, in that first coming, he was only "a babe wrapped in swaddling
cloths and lying in a manger" (Luke 2:12).

He could have taken another approach if he had wanted to.
Think of the tremendous energy he could have released. Think

of the light he could have produced, a trillion times brighter than the brightest stars. Think of the heat he could have generated, a trillion times hotter than the center of the sun. All earth's nuclear energy put together is just a few scraps of kindling wood compared to the explosive force that will usher in his final return. Let us not, therefore, mistake the simplicity of the babe for weakness. It is *God* who is "laid in the manger."

This divine condescension prompted St. Bernard of Clairvaux to ask, "Lord, what made you so small?" And his ecstatic response was, "It was *love!*"

The angels said to the shepherds, "Here are the tidings of great joy! We bring you good news!"

What is the good news? St. John put it succinctly in his marvelous formula: "The Word was made flesh."

In becoming a member of the human family, Christ established a relationship with every man and every woman. In joining the human family to himself, he has taken every member to himself. The whole cosmos has been transformed by the Word made flesh. The whole creation has become his body. He is the leaven that transforms everything into himself. The energy of the divine-human being is directed to one thing: to win our love. The light of all the galaxies points to one thing — his love for *us!* All the beauty, goodness, and truth in the world are designed to win our hearts to himself. Everything that exists is for us!

What is the secret of the divine energy encapsuled in the heart of the babe of Bethlehem? It is *Love!*

"Lord! Almighty and Eternal God! What makes you so tiny?"

Divine Love reaching out to each of us whoever we are.

18

CHRISTIAN ENLIGHTENMENT

The next day [John the Baptist] saw Jesus coming toward him and said, "Behold, the Lamb of God, who takes away the sin of the world. He is the one of whom I said, 'A man is coming after me who ranks ahead of me because he existed before me.' I did not know him but the reason why I came baptizing with water was that he might be made known to Israel." John testified further, saying, "I saw the Spirit come down like a dove from the sky and remain upon him. I did not know him, but the one who sent me to baptize with water told me, 'On whomever you see the Spirit come down and remain, he is the one who will baptize with the holy Spirit.' Now I have seen and testified that he is the Son of God." (John 1:29–34)

We are in the midst of the Christmas/Epiphany season. To understand this, it might be helpful to compare the great season from Advent to the Purification of the Virgin Mary to a five-act play in the Shakespearean model. I venture to say that Shakespeare got many of his ideas from the scriptures and the liturgy. In any case, a five-act Shakespearean play usually places the climax in the third act, so if you go home after the second act, you might as well not have come.

Act I of the unfolding Christmas/Epiphany mystery play begins with Advent. The feast of Christmas is the second act. There is an explosion of light in which the Eternal Word of God appears in his delightful humanity in the manger.

Epiphany is the third act. It tells us what this explosion of light contains. The value of light is in perceiving what it reveals. This is the knowledge that the feast of the Epiphany provides. It is the climax of the Christmas/Epiphany mystery.

In Act IV the baptism of Jesus in the river Jordan takes place. Act V is the marriage feast of Cana. Each of these events, although historical, is arranged by the liturgy to reveal the transcendent dimension of the Christmas/Epiphany Mystery. It is the celebration of divine light and its transmission.

Epiphany is the celebration of Christian enlightenment. In the liturgy, the historical events expressing this theme are juxtaposed: the coming of the magi, the baptism of Jesus in the Jordan, and the marriage feast of Cana. Through the celebration of these historical events, three important moments of grace are celebrated. The first is the revelation of the divinity of Jesus to the gentiles. The second is the revelation of the divinity of Jesus to his own people. The third is the revelation of the divinity of Jesus to his apostles and, through them, to us.

The call of the magi indicates the remote call to divine union addressed to every member of the human family in virtue of the Word becoming flesh.

Jesus' baptism in the Jordan is the proximate call to divine union in which we are invited to commit ourselves to the Gospel.

The marriage feast at Cana, especially the changing of water into wine, symbolizes the transformation of human nature into the divine, and the mystical marriage of those who have heard the call of the Gospel, followed it, and entered into divine union.

The full meaning of Acts IV and V of the Christmas/Epiphany drama is that those who have accepted baptism are incorporated into the body of Christ. They have heard the remote call to all humanity, accepted faith in Jesus, and are on the way to divine union. They are living cells in the body of Christ.

In this Gospel text "rest" is a key word. Actually, the Greek word means not just rest, but permanent rest. We get up after physical rest, but this rest accompanies us into action. The Spirit descends upon us in baptism, confirmation, and every time we receive the

Eucharist. The Spirit remains with us, transforming the material of daily life into experience of the divine.

The first level of rest is freedom from deliberate sin. Sin produces alienation, guilt, turmoil, distress. Hence it is not a space where the Spirit can rest. It is like inviting someone to rest on a bed covered with spikes. The first movement of the Spirit is to give us rest from deliberate sin. Jesus had no sin; hence the Spirit easily descended upon him. The Spirit descends less easily into the members of his body. Purification is necessary for this transforming process to reach its term.

The second level of rest is freedom from the inclination to sin. Purification is addressed not so much to personal sin but to its source, which is the false self with its self-centered programs for happiness that cannot possibly work. The capital sins are not actual sins but tendencies to prefer ourselves in the face of other people's needs.

The third level of rest is freedom from the false self. The ultimate rest is the rest of perfect love in which the self as a stable point of reference is transcended. Divine love expands our privatized horizons beyond our desires and ego trips.

Epiphany is an anticipation of Christ's passion, death, and resurrection (his decent into the waters of the Jordan and rising out of them). It celebrates our experience of purification and the unloading of the unconscious. It is our participation in the baptism of Jesus. We emerge from the dark and tumultuous waters of purification into the permanent rest of the Spirit.

19

THE UNFOLDING OF THE LIGHT

*And this is what he proclaimed: "One mightier than I is coming
after me, of whom I am not worthy to stoop and loosen the thongs
of his sandals. I have baptized you with water; he will baptize
you with the holy Spirit."*

*It happened in those days that Jesus came from Nazareth of
Galilee and was baptized in the Jordan by John. On coming up out
of the water he saw the heavens being torn open and the Spirit,
like a dove, descending upon him. And a voice came from the
heavens, "You are my beloved Son; with you I am well pleased."*

(Mark 1:7–13)

This liturgical period is the celebration of divine light and its
transmission. Let me review the basic stages of this unfolding of
the divine light and its transmission in the Christmas/Epiphany
mystery.

In Advent we celebrate the union of the Eternal Word of God
with human nature in the womb of the Virgin Mary. At Christmas
we celebrate the appearance of the Eternal Word of God in human
form as the babe in a manger. At Epiphany we celebrate the manifestation of the divinity of Jesus in the babe. Today at the baptism
in the Jordan, we celebrate the purification of the human family
so that it might be transformed and participate in the divine consciousness. The ultimate purpose of Christ's coming is to enable
each of us to assimilate the divine light that is being diffused over
the world during this liturgical season.

To understand this movement, let us look at one of the events that the liturgy relates to the transmission of divine light. The magi were astrologers in search of the truth. They stand for genuine seekers of the truth throughout the ages. The question arises, "What is the meaning of the historical event?" Everyone in the human family is invited to the banquet of divine love in virtue of God becoming a human being. Through faith we accept this remote call to divine union. This is the spiritual meaning of the historical event. As the light of faith grows brighter, we perceive the meaning of the event for us as individuals and begin to experience the unfolding of the stages of faith leading to divine union. Thus, the coming of the magi presents us with a panoramic view of what the divine light is revealing at this sacred season.

Today we are celebrating the baptism of Jesus in the Jordan. There is obviously no historical connection of this event with the coming of the magi, but the liturgy perceives this feast as a further manifestation of the divinity of Christ. It is a revelation of the Word made flesh to the Israelites. The Spirit descends upon Christ in the form of a dove as he submits to John's baptism, revealing the Eternal Word of God in human form to the Chosen People. The spiritual meaning of the event is that all who have accepted the invitation to divine union, and thus made the remote call proximate, participate in the anointing of Christ by the Spirit. Its spiritual significance for us is that we participate in the purifying waters of the Jordan, sanctified by Christ's touch, by exercising our faith in all the difficulties of life, within or without.

The other historical event celebrated in the feast of the Epiphany is the marriage feast of Cana. This event suggests the intimacy of divine union under the symbol of marriage. The marriage feast of Cana, at which Jesus changed water into wine, is loaded with spiritual significance. First of all, the historical event was the revelation of Christ to his closest followers. The Gospel says, "They saw his power and believed in him." The spiritual significance of the event is the consummation of the marriage of Christ to human nature in those who have heard the remote call, made it proximate by the acceptance of faith, and entered into divine union as a personal experience. This is the goal of the Gospel. It is not merely a historical document. It is a spiritual document with an interior dynamism that moves us as we exercise our faith into a view that penetrates all appearances. The full development of faith is the accessing of the divine presence within us and submitting to its transforming power. The Spirit of God, present in Christ, begins to manifest in us. We make the grace of Christ's incarnation, passion, death, and resurrection actual by our consent. Today, the grace of Epiphany enlightens our understanding so that we can accept our purification as a participation in the baptism of Christ.

20

THE WISDOM OF PARADOX

When the days were completed for their purification according to the law of Moses, they took him up to Jerusalem to present him to the Lord, just as it is written in the law of the Lord, "Every male that opens the womb shall be consecrated to the Lord," and to offer the sacrifice of "a pair of turtledoves or two young pigeons," in accordance with the dictate in the law of the Lord.

When they had fulfilled all the prescriptions of the law of the Lord, they returned to Galilee, to their own town of Nazareth. The child grew and became strong, filled with wisdom; and the favor of God was upon him. (Luke 2:22–24, 39–40)

The child grew in wisdom. Jesus is primarily a wisdom teacher and belongs to the tradition of the great wisdom teachers from earliest times. We believe Jesus Christ to be the complete expression of wisdom. Paul says, "In him are contained bodily all the wisdom and treasures of the Godhead." A wisdom teacher talks in paradoxes. What such a teacher says can never be interpreted literally, but only in the silence where the space from which the wisdom teacher speaks opens up within us. Only at the level of interior silence can we fully hear wisdom teaching.

Jesus teaches by word and example. In the crib he has only a few boo-hoo's to offer; nothing intelligible. Here is the first paradox: infinite power is power-less. But be careful! This child, so tender and mild, is dynamite. He is a time bomb. Just as we feel attracted to tickle him under the chin because he is so cute — "Poof!" —

our values are blasted to smithereens. What the child in the crib teaches by example and which he later speaks about undermines our personal attitudes, value systems, and behavior. The teaching of his example, vastly more powerful than all of Jesus' words put together, culminates in the cross, the ultimate powerlessness. It is the movement of human consciousness into unlimited being. This is the example this wisdom teacher invites us to emulate. The Gospel of Jesus is not about platitudes; it is not about right conduct for respectable citizens. It does not repudiate their virtues, but it questions the motivation they have for practicing them.

In the teaching of Jesus, true power is powerlessness. The greatest security is to have none. The purest hope is in the midst of hopelessness. True faith is full of doubts. And true love is nothing but service and, indeed, service unto death.

21

THE HIDDEN LIFE

Such was his intention when, behold, the angel of the Lord appeared to him in a dream and said, "Joseph, son of David, do not be afraid to take Mary your wife into your home. For it is through the holy Spirit that this child has been conceived in her."

(Matthew 1:20)

Catholic piety speaks of Joseph as the exemplar of the "hidden life," implying that this kind of life is of great value. If it is of great value, it must be because there is something about it that imitates God. In fact, God does seem to have a preference for concealment. God hides behind secondary causes and lets creatures get credit for what God actually is doing.

God also likes to hide his friends. God likes to hide them from the attention and acclaim of others and, above all, from themselves.

The hidden life takes many forms. In religious communities, the common life is a means of practicing the hidden life. In the apostolic way of life, external trials, rejection, and failure are means of doing the same thing. The wear and tear and ups and downs of marriage and family life are other means. The anonymity of oppressive circumstances is still another way. To be just a number in a jail, on a welfare role, or in a social security file; just another case for a social worker; to grow up and die in squalid circumstances where everybody is struggling for the bare necessities of life; or to endure a dog-eat-dog existence in the jungle of a ghetto — all these situations may conceal persons of extraordinary faith and love. The most beautiful flowers sometime blossom on a dump.

For the hidden life to do its work, one must accept and cheerfully accomplish the routine of ever-recurring duties and failures where nothing new ever seems to happen. The hidden life, in other words, is primarily a disposition. It is aimed directly at human pride, especially those religious pretensions that tempt us to make a splash in some pond or other. In Jesus' temptations in the desert, Satan tempted him to become a pious celebrity. Jesus' reply indicated that it is interior actions, much more than exterior actions, that really count. In order to turn us in this direction, God places us in circumstances that contradict, erode, or demolish our ambitions for ephemeral greatness.

Joseph appears as an important figure in the preparation of the Gospel. His marriage to the Virgin Mary seems to modify God's original commandment to Adam and Eve "to increase and multiply and fill the earth," giving that commandment a much broader meaning. In the marriage bond between Mary and Joseph, God seems to be extending an invitation to the human family to fill the earth in a *qualitative* manner — "to increase and multiply and fill the earth" with the experience of divine union and the full development of the power to love which that union brings about. The marriage of Joseph and Mary signifies this new understanding, for it was their spiritual union and not their physical union that brought the Son of man into the world and created the milieu in which he grew to maturity.

Some are surprised that Joseph never said anything in the Gospel. What could he say? The eternal Father spoke only one Word, which is his eternal Son. He has nothing further to say. Could the foster father of this Son say anything more? Jesus himself is the whole of Joseph's communication.

22

JESUS, THE LIGHT OF THE WORLD

As he passed by, he saw a man blind from birth. His disciples asked him, "Rabbi, who sinned, this man or his parents, that he was born blind?" Jesus answered, "Neither he nor his parents sinned; it is so that the works of God might be made visible through him. We have to do the works of the one who sent me while it is day. Night is coming when no one can work. While I am in the world, I am the light of the world." When he had said this, he spat on the ground and made clay with the saliva, and smeared the clay on his eyes, and said to him, "Go wash in the Pool of Siloam" (which means Sent). So he went and washed, and came back able to see.

His neighbors and those who had seen him earlier as a beggar said, "Isn't this the one who used to sit and beg?" Some said, "It is," but others said, "No, he just looks like him." He said, "I am." So they said to him, "[So] how were your eyes opened?" He replied, "The man called Jesus made clay and anointed my eyes and told me, 'Go to Siloam and wash.' So I went there and washed and was able to see." And they said to him, "Where is he?" He said, "I don't know."

They brought the one who was once blind to the Pharisees. Now Jesus had made clay and opened his eyes on a sabbath. So then the Pharisees also asked him how he was able to see. He said to them, "He put clay on my eyes, and I washed, and now I can see." So some of the Pharisees said, "This man is not from God, because he does not keep the sabbath." [But] others said, "How can a sinful man do such signs?" And there was a division among them. So they said to the blind man again, "What do you have to say about him, since he opened your eyes?" He said, "He is a prophet."

Now the Jews did not believe that he had been blind and gained his sight until they summoned the parents of the one who had gained his sight. They asked them, "Is this your son, who you say was born blind? How does he now see?" His parents answered and said, "We know that this is our son and that he was born blind. We do not know how he sees now, nor do we know who opened his eyes. Ask him, he is of age; he can speak for himself." His parents said this because they were afraid of the Jews, for the Jews had already agreed that if anyone acknowledged him as the Messiah, he would be expelled from the synagogue. For this reason his parents said, "He is of age; question him."

So a second time they called the man who had been blind and said to him, "Give God the praise! We know that this man is a sinner." He replied, "If he is a sinner, I do not know. One thing I do know is that I was blind and now I see." So they said to him, "What did he do to you? How did he open your eyes?" He answered them, "I told you already and you did not listen. Why do you want to hear it again? Do you want to become his disciples, too?" They ridiculed him and said, "You are that man's disciple; we are disciples of Moses! We know that God spoke to Moses, but we do not know where this one is from." The man answered and said to them, "This is what is so amazing, that you do not know where he is from, yet he opened my eyes. We know that God does not listen to sinners, but if one is devout and does his will, he listens to him. It is unheard of that anyone ever opened the eyes of a person born blind. If this man were not from God, he would not be able to do anything." They answered and said to him, "You were born totally in sin, and are you trying to teach us?" Then they threw him out.

When Jesus heard that they had thrown him out, he found him and said, "Do you believe in the Son of Man?" He answered

and said, "Who is he, sir, that I may believe in him?" Jesus said to
him, "You have seen him and the one speaking with you is he."
He said, "I do believe, Lord," and he worshiped him. Then Jesus
said, "I came into this world for judgment, so that those who do
not see might see, and those who do see might become blind."

Some of the Pharisees who were with him heard this and
said to him, "Surely we are not also blind, are we?" Jesus said to
them, "If you were blind, you would have no sin; but now you
are saying, 'We see,' so your sin remains." (John 9:1–41)

The fourth Sunday of Lent obviously deals with the theme
of Jesus Christ as the light of the world. This theological idea is
expressed in an incident in which the power of Jesus as light is
manifested.

This man was born blind as a result of the physical uncertain-
ties of the human condition. On the spiritual plane, the human
condition does not have the light to perceive what true happiness
is, although it has the potentiality and, indeed, an insatiable desire
for unlimited, boundless happiness. Seeing this man, Jesus with
his divine sensitivity was moved by the acute similarity between
this man's affliction and that of the human family that he had been
sent to redeem.

He looks at the blind man and sees a representative of the
poignant human predicament. Not knowing what happiness is is
the primary consequence of what is known as the Fall, experiencing
God as absent. The substance of all that we mean by the Fall refers
to the experience of growing up without the concomitant awareness of intimacy with God. That relationship is the true security,
the true happiness. The human predicament consists in trying to
cope with the absence of true happiness and our inability to find
out what it is and how to find it. The purpose of religion is to enable
us to reconnect. Religion means to bind back, to put back together,
to bond us to God and to God's faithful love.

To look at this blind man begging for food is for Jesus an acute
pain. Naturally he wants to do something about it. Notice what he
does. He spits on the ground. We read in the scriptures that Yahweh
breathed the breath of life into the first man. Jesus also breathed

on his disciples after his resurrection, bestowing upon them the fullness of the Spirit.

Breathing is a symbol of the bestowal of the Spirit (The word "Spirit" means breath). Saliva also represents the bestowal of the Spirit. Jesus mixes his spittle with dirt making a mud-pie. He then anoints the eyes of the blind man with the mud, symbolizing the Incarnation of the Word made flesh.

The text points to the healing of the human predicament, which is seeking happiness in the wrong places. Happiness is re-bonding with the divine presence and action within.

A new dimension has been introduced into the human family. Not only is divine intimacy restored but infinitely more is given. This is why the liturgy describes Adam's fall as a "happy fault." It calls forth a mercy that was greater than the original gift. The last state is much more marvelous than the first. Human brokenness and sinfulness become the springboard into glory. As Paul says, "When I am weak, then I am strong." Or to paraphrase, "When I accept my nothingness, then I am everything."

Easter is the superabundant joy in the new gift of God that transcends the original plan. God himself becomes part of the human family in order that we may participate in the divine life, not as something given from outside, but as something that inherently belongs to us as human beings through solidarity with Jesus Christ. This idea of solidarity with God through Jesus Christ, the divine human being, describes the mystical intuition of the unity of the human family.

Think back to that great event in the early 1960s when, for the first time, a human being set foot on the moon. Maybe you watched the astronaut stepping out of the space capsule and imprinting on the dusty surface of the moon a human footprint. I remember the headline, "MAN REACHES THE MOON." Something shifted in everybody's psyche at that moment. As that man's foot touched the moon, there was a sense that the human family was suddenly in a different place. In virtue of our solidarity as a single species, we all graduated from our earthbound straitjacket and took our first step into the universe beyond our earthbound horizons. In that event the human family was unified by a footprint.

The Gospel bears witness to an event that, rightly understood, could unify the human family. St. John's belated headline reads, "And the Word was made flesh and dwelt among us." What could be more sensational or bigger news? God has become a human being.

23

THE GREAT I AM

"Amen, amen, I say to you, whoever keeps my word will never see death." [So] the Jews said to him, "Now we are sure that you are possessed. Abraham died, as did the prophets, yet you say, 'Whoever keeps my word will never taste death.' Are you greater than our father Abraham, who died? Or the prophets, who died? Who do you make yourself out to be?" Jesus answered, "If I glorify myself, my glory is worth nothing; but it is my Father who glorifies me, of whom you say, 'He is our God.' You do not know him, but I know him. And if I should say that I do not know him, I would be like you a liar. But I do know him and I keep his word. Abraham your father rejoiced to see my day; he saw it and was glad. So the Jews said to him, "You are not yet fifty years old and you have seen Abraham?" Jesus said to them, "Amen, amen, I say to you, before Abraham came to be, I AM." So they picked up stones to throw at him; but Jesus hid and went out of the temple area. (John 8:51–59)

This text is one of the last exchanges between Jesus and the civil and religious leaders of Jerusalem. When Jesus speaks of himself in the kind of terminology that God had used to identify himself at the burning bush, naturally the people feel uncomfortable. When Moses pressed Yahweh for his name, he replied, "I AM Who Am," or "I AM That I AM." Jesus points to the inner mystery of his own being, which is about to be revealed in his passion, death, resurrection, and ascension.

We cannot speak of Jesus' inner being without confronting our own. Christian faith tells us that Jesus has so taken the human family to himself that he is present in every human being past, present, and to come. This is the revelation that John unveils in the Prologue to his Gospel when he writes, "In the beginning was the Word and the Word was with God and the Word was God" (John 1:1). Out of the infinite silence of Ultimate Reality emerges the Eternal Word, expressing all that is contained in that silence, which is infinite potentiality and actuality. This interior Word of God, Creator of all that exists, entered creation as a human being. Paul writes in Colossians, "In him all the fullness of the Godhead resides" (Col. 1:20). "All things were created in him and for him" (Col. 1:17).

When we hear the words, "Before Abraham was created, I AM," coming from the lips of a human being, we are in the presence of a great mystery. No one else ever made such a claim. "I AM" implies being without limit. Can a finite human being be infinite potentiality? Jesus says, "I AM." He could make that statement only if he was in possession of all that the Father is.

Jesus in his divine nature is, in Paul's words, *THE CHRIST*, that is, the Eternal Word of God. This creative energy is the source of our life at every level and might be called the divine ground of our being. According to one significant hypothesis (Michael Washburn, *The Ego and the Divine Ground*), each of us in our early childhood represses this divine ground. In biblical tradition this notion of a primordial loss of innocence is conveyed in the event of the Fall. A powerful truth is struggling to be expressed in the story of Adam and Eve. The innocence of childhood, which we all experienced for a time, is the enjoyment of reality without reflection. The child enjoys seeing as seeing, hearing as hearing, touching as touching, tasting as tasting, smelling as smelling. It has not developed a discriminating mind. God is seeing through the child's eyes; smelling with the child's nose; speaking in its baby talk; walking with its baby feet. There is no separation between the child's experience of life and its ground of being. Hence, the sheer delight that an infant manifests on occasion.

Once the repression of the divine ground of being occurs, the infant develops an awareness of himself or herself as distinct from other objects. The separate-self sense increases until the child arrives at full reflective self-consciousness around the age of reason. We could not develop our own personality or mental ego without repressing our divine ground. Once this process begins, the developing ego keeps the divine ground out of awareness, and its energy is reduced to sustaining bodily life, while the psyche goes on developing without the sense of union with its source. We experience ourselves as subjects over and against other objects. A lingering sense of loss remains, however, for our former innocence.

In light of Jesus' identification as "the Word that enlightens everyone that comes into the world," we might say that God is the great repression and that that repression is de-repressed in the spiritual journey. Jesus said, "I am the way, the truth, and the life." As the way, he shows us how to live human life divinely. This is the project that Paul called the mystery that has been hidden from the beginning of time and that is revealed in Christ. Christ is the ground of our being and source of the divine energy that is transforming us. As the Incarnate Word, he calls us to repentance — to change the direction in which we are looking for happiness. The programs of the false self must be exchanged for the values of the Gospel that lead to integration with the divine ground.

Why did God permit this original repression? In the liturgy of Holy Saturday the Fall is described as "a happy fault." One thing that is good is that this repression has enabled us to develop all the talents that are inherent in our particular human nature so that, once this rerooting is completed, all our human experience is at the service of the divine ground. The Spirit can work in human affairs in a way that would not have been possible if we had remained in the state of innocence.

Suppose that you are on the spiritual journey and are practicing some nonconceptual meditation that is opening you to the presence of God within you. The genius of the Christian tradition is that it identifies the divine ground as "Abba," "Father" — as benign, loving, and protective. All the symbols in the psalms that call God "rock," "fortress," "strong tower" are symbols of protection. They are concrete experiences of this energy.

If the divine ground is the core of our being and the source of our life at every moment, it is impossible to be separated from God. The thought that we are separate is the great illusion. We think we are separate; we feel we are separate; hence, we *act* as though we are separate. That is the "fall." That is its chief consequence. That attitude is the root of all sin — the frantic effort to find satisfaction or to get away from intolerable frustration even if this involves trampling on other people's rights and needs.

Suppose that we are established in our own personal identity by a strong ego in the psychological sense. In the spiritual journey this begins to disintegrate. Our emotional programs for happiness are undermined by the night of sense, a well-documented stage in the spiritual journey, which St. John of the Cross believes is common among those who commit themselves whole-heartedly to a life of prayer. The light that God sheds on those emotional programs reveals their selfishness and convinces us intuitively that only God can give perfect happiness. This intuition relativizes all that we hoped would give us happiness. Naturally, we go into a period of mourning. The night of sense is not a rejection of anything created. It is not a repression in any sense of the term. It is simply the realization that creatures, good as they are, cannot provide us with the unlimited happiness for which our spirit is designed. The divine presence secretly insinuates itself into our consciousness and undermines the props that support our false self. If we do not have any knowledge of this presence, we may be frightened, uneasy, and confused. Every now and then there may come a rush of this energy into our consciousness and we are blown away. This could be an awesome or frightening experience because we are so out of touch with our true self that we do not know what it is; and when it begins to manifest itself, we realize that it is going to undermine the fragile infrastructure that we call our personality. So we may get spooked and run away from this energy. We are afraid to be quiet because we are afraid to meet it face to face.

Things we have repressed that were frightening in early childhood easily cling to it. If we were afraid of the dark, the unknown, or the boogie man or are now afraid of losing control, this unexpected intruder into our consciousness can be terrifying. That reaction is not because the energy is terrifying in itself, but because we do not know what it is and have no conceptual background to prepare us for this kind of experience. To know that Christ is speaking to us in the Gospel and that he is coming to us in the sacraments precisely to awaken that energy is an enormous encouragement. When we say, "Come Lord Jesus, come," we should be aware that he does not have far to come, and that if he comes, our world will come to an end. Our world is shattered by every existential confrontation, however brief, with the Ultimate Reality.

At the same time, this is an incredible invitation. If we can make friends with this unknown intruder, we return little by little to the innocence of childhood. When Jesus said, "Unless you become like little children, you cannot enter the Kingdom of God," he did not mean the destruction of the ego as such. He meant the destruction of the false self. The beatitudes heal each level of primitive consciousness through which we have passed, preserving what is good and bringing the distortions and exaggerations to an end. In this way, all of our human experience can be placed at the service of the divine ground, Christ within us.

Christ-consciousness is the return to our Source. We have received far more than was lost by the Fall. The repression of the divine presence is "the sin of the world." That is what Christ came to heal; not just this or that sin, but the source of all sin, which is alienation from God. Hence, it is essential in our practice to remind ourselves again and again that God and we cannot be separated. He sees the world out of our eyes; God works through our hands; God speaks through our voice; God walks on our feet. He is even present in our sins. This is why we should not subject God to the indignities that our sins involve. We are temples of the Holy Spirit according to Paul. Our bodies are holy because they are lived in by God.

Baptism is a commitment to death and resurrection. The death of what? Not the body, obviously, because it lives on. Baptism is the commitment to the death of the false self. The first stage of our spiritual journey is rocky because the energy of the divine ground is not controllable. We have to accept it on its own terms. The false-self system is the controlling, security-seeking, approval-seeking self. That is the self that must die. Nothing that is good on any of the levels of consciousness up to and including the use of reason is lost. The first part of the journey is bound to be experienced as the destruction of our worldview and self-image, the uprooting and tearing down, the boring from within and the battering from without. We feel like a wreck. We are a wreck. God is tearing down the old tenement (the false self) brick by brick. Paul says it has not entered the mind of anybody what God has prepared for those who love him. The return to innocence is where we are heading, all evidence to the contrary notwithstanding.

Do not believe the false-self commentary that says, "I'm hopeless. My mind won't be quiet. I can't let go of my need to control." The divine ground, once we submit and surrender to it, is constantly hacking away at the false self with pickaxe and shovel. That is when we start shouting, "Leave me in my sins; I'm happier with them! Anything is better than this!"

It is only the false self that is squealing. "We are like sheep led to the slaughter." The false self feels that it is being skinned alive or torn to pieces. And there are no tranquilizers or sedatives for this process. Once we have made friends with the divine ground and identified it as Christ, we have the motivation to entrust ourselves to this mysterious power. Every now and then the energy of the ground bursts out in unexpected ways, creating confusion of mind. We have to face once again the instinctual needs of the child in the form of the libido, anger, and fear, because God is also the source of those energies. The repressive apparatus began in infancy. Thus, as we are rerooted in our source, there may be upsurges of energy that are hard to control. Instinctual needs that we thought we had gained control over in earlier periods of our lives resurface. Actually, it was the controlling apparatus of the mental ego that kept things fairly respectable. Now we are confronted with the raw stuff. We are ready to run away or look for some better way of getting to heaven. But there is no better way. We have to accept all the energies of the divine ground. Little by little they are integrated into the other values of human nature.

Then begins the second phase of the journey, which might be called resurrection. The dark, frightening, and accusing energy becomes delightful, sweet, and full of love. Even though we do not always understand what Jesus is saying, his external words awaken the divine presence within. The divine word within is the same as the divine word without. They mutually confirm one another. The word of God in scripture awakens the divine ground within. As faith and trust wake up, divine love wakes up, too. Christ, so to speak, rolls over within us. We are finally ready to submit our lives totally to the guidance of our source.

This is the project that is being celebrated during Lent. Hence, Lent can be painful and filled with temptation. At Easter we celebrate the return of innocence and the integration of all our human experience into the divine ground of our being. Union with the divine life is restored, only now on a much grander scale. Instead of the limitations of childhood, the whole development of the human organism and the mental ego with all its talents are now available to the divine energy. This would not have been possible had we not first experienced the Fall, now perceived to be "a happy fault."

24

THE DEATH OF LAZARUS

Now a man was ill, Lazarus from Bethany, the village of Mary and her sister Martha. Mary was the one who had anointed the Lord with perfumed oil and dried his feet with her hair; it was her brother Lazarus who was ill. So the sisters sent word to him, saying, "Master, the one you love is ill." When Jesus heard this he said, "This illness is not to end in death, but is for the glory of God, that the Son of God may be glorified through it." Now Jesus loved Martha and her sister and Lazarus. So when he heard that he was ill, he remained for two days in the place where he was. Then after this he said to his disciples, "Let us go back to Judea." The disciples said to him, "Rabbi, the Jews were just trying to stone you, and you want to go back there?" Jesus answered, "Are there not twelve hours in a day? If one walks during the day, he does not stumble, because he sees the light of this world. But if one walks at night, he stumbles, because the light is not in him." He said this, and then told them, "Our friend Lazarus is asleep, but I am going to awaken him." So the disciples said to him, "Master, if he is asleep, he will be saved." But Jesus was talking about his death, while they thought that he meant ordinary sleep. So then Jesus said to them clearly, "Lazarus has died. And I am glad for you that I was not there, that you may believe. Let us go to him." So Thomas, called Didymus, said to his fellow disciples, "Let us also go to die with him."

When Jesus arrived, he found that Lazarus had already been in the tomb for four days. Now Bethany was near Jerusalem, only about two miles away. And many of the Jews had come to Martha and Mary to comfort them about their brother. When Martha heard that Jesus was coming, she went to meet him; but Mary sat at home. Martha said to Jesus, "Lord, if you had been here, my brother would not have died. [But] even now I know that whatever you ask of God, God will give you." Jesus said to her, "Your brother will rise." Martha said to him, "I know he will rise, in the resurrection on the last day." Jesus told her, "I am the resurrection and the life; whoever believes in me, even if he dies, will live, and everyone who lives and believes in me will never die. Do you believe this?" She said to him, "Yes, Lord. I have come to believe that you are the Messiah, the Son of God, the one who is coming into the world."

When she had said this, she went and called her sister Mary secretly, saying, "The teacher is here and is asking for you." As soon as she heard this, she rose quickly and went to him. For Jesus had not yet come into the village, but was still where Martha had met him. So when the Jews who were with her in the house comforting her saw Mary get up quickly and go out, they followed her, presuming that she was going to the tomb to weep there. When Mary came to where Jesus was and saw him, she fell at his feet and said to him, "Lord, if you had been here, my brother would not have died." When Jesus saw her weeping and the Jews who had come with her weeping, he became perturbed and deeply troubled, and said, "Where have you laid him?" They said to him, "Sir, come and see." And Jesus wept. So the Jews said, "See how he loved him." But some of them said, "Could not the one who opened the eyes of the blind man have done something so that this man would not have died?"

So Jesus, perturbed again, came to the tomb. It was a cave, and a stone lay across it. Jesus said, "Take away the stone." Martha, the dead man's sister, said to him, "Lord, by now there will be a stench; he has been dead for four days." Jesus said to her, "Did I not tell you that if you believe you will see the glory of God?"

So they took away the stone. And Jesus raised his eyes and said,
"Father, I thank you for hearing me. I know that you always hear
me; but because of the crowd here I have said this, that they may
believe that you sent me." And when he had said this, he cried
out in a loud voice, "Lazarus, come out!" The dead man came out,
tied hand and foot with burial bands, and his face was wrapped
in a cloth. So Jesus said to them, "Untie him and let him go."

(John 11:1–45)

This Gospel points to the basic theme of the Lenten observance, which is death and resurrection. What dies and what rises during this season of grace?

First of all, what strikes us as strange is Jesus' lack of response to the poignant requests of Lazarus's sisters. Actually, they didn't really ask for anything. It is characteristic of great love to be interested primarily in God's will. The sisters did not write, "Lord, please cure our brother." They simply stated the problem: "The one whom you love is ill." They laid their concern in front of Jesus and let him decide what to do. They had graduated from the tendency to advise God as to how God should run things by doing what they wanted. Although Jesus had cured many people even though he had never even seen them before, for Lazarus, his dear friend, he did nothing. In fact, "he stayed just where he was for two more days," allowing Lazarus's illness to run its full course, ending with his death.

What does this event signify for us? It suggests that this illness of Lazarus was of a special character. It was not just the flu or any old disease. In the context of Lent the church clearly sees it as an image of the consequences of the human condition (original sin), and the only cure for this disease is death. The illness of Lazarus consisted in his becoming fully aware of just how sick he was. Interior purification, in which the Spirit excavates the emotional damage of our personal history layer by layer, is to experience this illness in all its force. As one experiences the more primitive emotions of early childhood, one feels as though one is getting sicker. The only cure for this illness is to allow it to run its full course. Lazarus's physical death becomes the symbol of the death of the false self.

Lazarus represents the human condition which Jesus has come to heal, not by plastering over its deep wounds, but by experiencing them just as they are.

The first step in the cure of any disease is to recognize that we have one and to want to be healed. We may be aware that there is something wrong in our motivation and behavior, but do we sincerely want to be cured? This is an important point. The need of healing is precisely what the contemplative life reveals. Our motivation to be healed is in direct proportion to our perception of how much the emotional programs for happiness are injuring our relationship with ourselves, God, and other people — how much, in other words, they are limiting our capacity to love God and to serve others.

The second step in the healing of the human condition is to accept the disease with all its immediate consequences: suffering, humiliation, failure, anxiety, and sense of alienation from God. This is the transition from our original conversion to a life of pure faith.

The third step is to accept all the possible consequences of the disease: the fact that it might last a long time, get worse, and lead to other complications.

The fourth step is to identify the disease and our inability to get over it as our share in the cross of Christ and to trust him for the grace to endure it without being discouraged.

The fifth step is to experience God's infinite mercy in the midst of the ever-increasing proof of our powerlessness.

The sixth step is to abandon ourselves completely to God, no longer caring about being cured so long as the disease does not offend God.

The seventh step is to abide in the midst of our powerlessness with unshakable confidence in God's boundless forgiveness and mercy. This is the attitude that enables us to accept the human condition just as it is and to await the inner resurrection of God's grace. Indeed, as we climb these steps, divine love enables us to work with ever-increasing energy in the service of others.

There are seven stages in Lazarus's resurrection, which correspond to the inner resurrection of the divine life in us.

1. The first stage of the awakening of Lazarus is his becoming conscious of his illness, the symbol of the exhaustion of all his efforts to get well. The stone sealing the tomb is the symbol of the false self, which keeps him locked into himself and his particular worldview.

2. The stone is rolled away admitting light, air, and warmth, symbols of the first stirrings of hope in the heart of one paralyzed by the false self.

3. Jesus calls Lazarus by name. In the scriptures this is the special indication of God's love, accepting him unconditionally just as he is.

4. Jesus commands Lazarus to come forth from his tomb, symbol of bursting the bonds of compulsion, evil habits, and addiction.

5. Lazarus staggers to the mouth of the tomb, bound hand and foot in the winding bands of his burial. He is still wrapped in the habits of the false self, unable to move freely in the new life that has begun in him, but which has not yet worked itself into all of his activities and relationships.

6. "Untie him and let him go." With these words Jesus communicates to Lazarus the full freedom of the children of God.

7. Finally Lazarus is seated at table with Jesus at Simon the leper's house, symbol of the celebration of the risen life of Christ that has now been communicated to him, enabling him to see God in all things and all things in God.

On the threshold of Holy Week this Gospel points to our experience of Lent as a renewed confrontation with our mixed motivation, weakness of will, and lingering bondage to the influences of our cultural conditioning and prepackaged values. Lent invites us to come forth from that bondage into the freedom that the resurrection of Jesus transmits to us and that is anticipated and symbolized in the resurrection of Lazarus.

25

LIGHT FROM LIGHT

If then, we have died with Christ, we believe that we shall also live with him. We know that Christ, raised from the dead, dies no more; death no longer has power over him. As to his death, he died to sin once and for all; as to his life, he lives for God. Consequently, you, too, must think of yourselves as [being] dead to sin and living for God in Christ Jesus. (Romans 6:8–11)

In the Paschal Vigil we participate in a movement from darkness into light, from silence into music, from subdued reverence into the bursting joy of the great Alleluia. A mysterious joy rises up irresistibly in our hearts as we perceive what Christ our Savior has done for us, is doing for us, will do for us. Christ, as Paul tells us, will be all in all in the end. But already his being all in all has begun with his resurrection. Baptism is witness to the fact that Christ has risen in our hearts. He is the true Self of everyone, expressing himself in each of us as he wills — or as much as we allow.

During the Paschal Vigil the light from the Paschal Candle spreads from candle to candle until the whole church is filled with light, symbolizing Christ rising in our hearts. He is alive in the center of our being as a tiny light with the power to spread through every faculty until our entire being is filled with light, and then through us to set the divine fire of love aflame everywhere in the world. Even though it looks as though this transformation is not happening in our own personal lives or in the world around us, faith in the risen Christ tells us that appearances are deceptive.

Christ has made us, as Paul said in the Epistle, "alive to God in Christ Jesus" (Rom. 6:11). Because Christ is our true Self, God can command us to do what humanly speaking is impossible: to love God with our whole mind, heart, strength, and will, and our neighbor as ourselves. We love ourselves because Christ is at our center. We must also recognize the same divine presence in each other. Christ is becoming all in all, loving himself in us and pouring into us and into the world the power of his resurrection. It is already here. It is available. Like the flame of the Paschal Candle, it is spreading.

But there is something more than awakening to the experience of Christ dwelling in our inmost being and in that of others. I refer to the new commandment Jesus promulgated at the Last Supper: "This is my commandment, that you love one another as I have loved you" (John 15:12).

He loves us because we share his being through the wonderful gift of creation and through the still more wonderful gift of his redeeming passion, death, and resurrection. He also loves us in our uniqueness, in our individuality, that is, in our limitations, weakness, and sinfulness. Paul, therefore, exhorts us to "bear one another's burdens . . . " (Gal. 6:2). This is the sign that divine love is abiding in us. God's unfailing love is irreversible. It waits; it bears with us. It is forgiving, accepting, inclines to serve. The ripe fruit of the grace of Easter is to share with one another the kind of forgiveness, acceptance, and service that Christ has shown to us. Christ being you, Christ being me, Christ being each one of us — such is the reality on which the commandment of love is based.

26

BEING TRULY PRESENT

On the evening of that first day of the week, when the doors were locked, where the disciples were, for fear of the Jews, Jesus came and stood in their midst and said to them, "Peace be with you." When he had said this, he showed them his hands and his side. The disciples rejoiced when they saw the Lord. [Jesus] said to them again, "Peace be with you. As the Father has sent me, so I send you." And when he had said this, he breathed on them and said to them, "Receive the holy Spirit. Whose sins you forgive are forgiven them, and whose sins you retain are retained."

(John 20:19–23)

The peace of the Lord is the supreme gift that is offered to us on this feast. Peace is something greater than joy or any emotion. It is beyond joy and beyond suffering. It is the rerooting of our entire being and self-identity in its Source so that the feeling of being separated from God is dissolved. There is no more feeling of separation from God once the grace of Pentecost has done its work.

Peace is defined as the tranquility of order: everything in its right place. The right order for human beings is to see, hear, touch, feel, and taste God in everything that happens. The Holy Spirit comes today to awaken us to the Beatitudes, which heal at each successive level of developing human consciousness whatever was limited and which bring the tranquility of order into our whole being. Thus, every value, both human and divine, is brought together in perfect simplicity and unity.

The Holy Spirit descended on the house where the disciples were gathered with such force that it was like a tornado or hurricane. Everyone in the neighborhood heard it and came running to the place saying, "What happened?" People from all over the world, present in Jerusalem on that day, heard the apostles speaking about the wonderful works of God in their own tongue. This is an image of what the transformation of Christian life is meant to be. It is an expression of the tranquility of our whole being in relationship not only to ourselves but to every living thing.

During the Pentecost event, the people heard God speaking to them in all the various languages of the earth. The grace of Pentecost enables us to hear God speaking in every human being and in every event. Thus everything outside and inside manifests the divine. The Beatitudes and the seven Gifts of the Spirit empower us to live at the cutting edge of God's presence and action. God is always present. In the past, we thought God was absent. That was the monumental illusion that made happiness impossible.

We live waiting for the right moment to be converted and to start to practice the virtues, to pray, or to enter some ministry. All of us are waiting for the perfect situation when at last we have the time for prayer, reflection, spiritual reading, service to others, when we can be reconciled with our disagreeable relatives, when we can forgive our enemies, our early education, the church, our mothers and fathers, and finally ourselves. This sad state of affairs must be changed, and it can be changed by allowing ourselves to see, feel, touch, taste, smell the divine presence right now. It is only our habit of not seeing God that stands in the way.

Until we live with reality in the present moment, we postpone it. Seeing the presence of Christ in the present moment is the way to transformation. This is what the grace of Pentecost will do if we work at it. Just say, "Here he comes! I embrace him — hidden in this trial, in this dreadful person, in this stomach ache, in this overwhelming joy." He is in the present moment no matter what the content of the moment is.

27

THE GIFT OF COUNSEL

*"If you love me, you will keep my commandments. And I will
ask the Father, and he will give you another Advocate to be with
you always, the Spirit of truth, which the world cannot accept,
because it neither sees nor knows it. But you know it, because it
remains with you, and will be in you. I will not leave you orphans;
I will come to you. In a little while, the world will no longer see
me, but you will see me, because I live and you will live. On that
day you will realize that I am in my Father and you are in me and
I in you. Whoever has my commandments and observes them is
the one who loves me. And whoever loves me will be loved by
my Father, and I will love him and reveal myself to him."*

(John 14:15–22)

   In the Gospel Jesus speaks of the Spirit as the "counselor." In
Jesus' time this was a legal assistant. The gift that disposes us to
be moved by this counselor is the gift of counsel that teaches us
how to find our path to God and how to stay on it. This marvelous
gift enables us to make decisions that are inspired by the Spirit not
only at decisive moments of life, but in the routine details of daily
living. The Spirit acts as a kind of nurse who instructs, consoles,
and nurtures. The divine mercy and goodness are communicated
through this super-person who guides us out of the swamp of the
human condition into participation in the divine life. Most of us
are too modest in our expectations of God. God is prepared to give
us the universe and we go for an anthill.

Notice the counselor, the Spirit, is not just *beside* us. Jesus said, "He will be within you." This is more than a partnership. To what can we compare it? The counseling that the Spirit gives is similar to the expertise of the best of psychotherapists. The Spirit assists us to acknowledge the truth of our human condition and to learn how to handle it. The spiritual journey is a therapeutic situation in the fullest sense of the word. The Spirit, through the gift of counsel, invites us to let go of the obstacles to the divine action. The first thing we have to do in order to be moved by another is to let go of our resistances and to cultivate the docility and trust necessary to be moved by this higher power. It is not enough to know the dark side of our personality, the shadow side. This material often discourages us instead of encourages us. Normally we don't see the growth of self-knowledge as the fruit of the divine therapy. Rather, we experience it as an attack on our self-esteem. Hence, we resist rather than submit to the knowledge that is leading to truth and to freedom.

The Spirit teaches us how to handle the humiliations of the false self. In contemplative prayer, the divine light uncovers the emotional pain of early life in the form of primitive emotions released spontaneously (although often painfully) during periods of prayer. This pain is a sign that the therapy is working. When the divine light reveals the trauma of early childhood, we may think it is the end of our spiritual journey. We may expect contemplative prayer to provide peace and consolation. It may at times provide consolation, but if that is all it provides, it is simply a tranquilizer that soothes upsetting feelings momentarily, but leaves all our problems in place. Hence, the necessity of welcoming the divine Spirit, as pointed out in this text, as the Spirit of truth. The Spirit of truth will not allow any cover-ups. When we have experienced sufficient bonding and transference with the Divine Therapist, we can face with courage the emotional pain of a lifetime. At this point, it is extremely important to recognize that the Spirit is pointing out our problems. In other words, when we experience a surge of envy, the need to be special, or to have someone show us special attention, this is the very best opportunity to welcome that knowledge. It is as if the Divine Therapist were saying, "Dear Soul, have a look at the source of this upsetting emotion. What are you afraid of? Let the feeling come up and welcome it, because this is the information you need to know in order to be free."

How to be free from this temptation? Pray to be free! "I turn over to you this need to be special. I let go of my jealousy toward those who seem to be getting the special attention that I want."

Our relationship with God is the essential ingredient of successful therapy. The feeling of alienation from God and the lack of the experience of the divine presence is the source of every neurosis and addiction. When an afflictive emotion arises, one simply looks at the Spirit, welcomes the information, and congratulates God on excavating this hidden secret. *"Oh, this jealousy, this anger, this guilt — I love it!"* But instead of identifying with it and acting it out, we give it to God. How different our attitude would be if we welcomed neurotic tendencies with honesty instead of seeing them as humiliations. Humility is the atmosphere in which we can be whoever we are without feeling bad. We are glad to be ourselves because now God can exercise his creativity and healing power. No one is excluded from the divine therapy except those who think they are well.

In prayer and in daily life, we are constantly encountering our neurotic tendencies. Are we running away from them or embracing them as part of our therapy?

To sum up, we need to learn from the Spirit how to perceive the dark stuff and how to deal with it. We handle it best by welcoming it, or at least by accepting it if we can't succeed right away in welcoming it. Then without analyzing or acting out our feelings, we pray to be free, and then act as if nothing had happened. In this way, the Spirit frees us from the emotional pain of a lifetime together with all the means of coping with it that have caused us to resist rather than trust the divine therapy.

"I will send you," Jesus said, "another Counselor, who will not just be with you, but will be within you, who will teach you all the truth." The truth is that we are in Christ and he is in God and God is in us. The goal of the divine therapy is the experience of the Trinitarian life opening up within us.

28

THE BODY OF CHRIST

At that time Jesus said, "I am the living bread that came down from heaven; whoever eats this bread will live forever; and the bread that I will give is my flesh for the life of the world."

The Jews quarreled among themselves, saying, "How can this man give us [his] flesh to eat?" Jesus said to them, "Amen, amen, I say to you, unless you eat the flesh of the Son of Man and drink his blood, you do not have life within you." Whoever eats my flesh and drinks my blood has eternal life, and I will raise him on the last day. For my flesh is true food, and my blood is true drink. Whoever eats my flesh and drinks my blood remains in me and I in him. Just as the living Father sent me and I have life because of the Father, so also the one who feeds on me will have life because of me. This is the bread that came down from heaven. Unlike your ancestors who ate and still died, whoever eats this bread will live forever." (John 6: 51–59)

We are celebrating the Feast of Corpus Christi, the Latin word for the body of Christ. This is the celebration of the Eucharist as one of the ripe fruits of the Pentecostal grace and the full flowering of Christ's redeeming death and resurrection. The human body as such is experiencing a renaissance in the West. As a result of advances in Western medicine and the arrival of Eastern medical ideas and practice, there is a resurgence of interest, respect, and concern with regard to the body. Obviously, since Christ had a human body, these new ideas are doors to enlarge our understanding of what Paul calls *the body of Christ*. One of these new ideas is holistic medicine. Its basic principle is that it is not enough to heal the physical body; we must also heal the mind and the spirit. In fact, if we don't do something about our mind and spirit, our symptoms are likely to return because the body is the manifestation of how we are on the mental level. Holistic medicine has been defined as the heath of body, mind, and spirit. The body-mind-spirit distinction is found in Paul and comes out of the Hebrew frame of reference.

The Eastern frame of reference is more comprehensive. In its view, we have a physical body, an etheric body, an emotional body, an astral body, a mental body, both high and low, and a spiritual body. The latter energizes and guides all these bodies. Thus, we are the same person manifesting God on different levels. In this frame of reference, energy in various forms can be present in the same space at different frequencies.

In the Hebrew frame of reference, which Western Christianity has inherited, we have simplified these levels to body, mind, and spirit. When we say that holistic health involves the above three, we might keep in mind this more expanded view of Eastern medicine.

With regard to Christ, his physical body stands for all the other manifestations of his divine Person. When we receive the Eucharist, we receive all the bodies of Christ including his glorified body. Holistic medicine for a Christian includes participation in the glorified body of Christ with his divinized human nature. This includes his experience of being in the Father and knowing the Father as the Ultimate Reality. The Eucharist brings us the seed of divine awareness, and hence a form of health beyond any category of which we can conceive. When we receive the Eucharist, we are appropriating the mind of Christ.

It is not just the mind of Christ that we receive. We also receive the Spirit of Christ. The Holy Spirit is communicated as a life to be lived and enjoyed and the pledge of that further health that is called glory, which is happiness beyond any conceivable category. It is a way of becoming God. Not that we become numerically one with God. Rather, we participate in the divine happiness that is unlimited truth and love. This is ultimate human health.

If in receiving the Eucharist we are taking into ourselves the mind of Christ with his dispositions, we will begin to function out of the various bodies of Christ. We will bring forth the fruits of the Spirit, the Beatitudes, and anticipate at times the glory that awaits us, but that the physical body is not capable of sustaining in this life. The divine action withholds the full force of its energy in this life so we are not burned to a crisp. It will be communicated when the limitations of our physical body slip away and our spiritual body emerges in the fullness of its potentiality. We will rise, according to Paul, in a spiritual body.

When we receive the body of Christ in this expanded sense, what should be our intention? Certainly not just to go through a ritual or to fulfil our Easter duty. Our intention must be to accept the body of Christ as it is and to consent to everything that it is. The body of Christ is victim, gift, and the source of health for the whole of humanity. Our intention must be solidarity with everyone in the human family, past, present, and to come. Receiving the Eucharist with this intention of identification with the mind of Christ is an infusion of enormous energy into the psychological atmosphere of the planet. Because of its inherent power, it can reach those places in the world that seem to be immersed in violence, hatred, and the very reverse of the mind of Christ. Satan is the symbol of all that is not the body of Christ. When the celebrant says, "the body of Christ," and we say, "Amen," we are identifying with Christ at each level of his being. Human health is our participation in the divine life anticipated in our physical bodies and to be completed in our glorified bodies.

29

THE DOUBLE BIND

When the time arrived for Elizabeth to have her child she gave birth to a son. Her neighbors and relatives heard that the Lord had shown his great mercy toward her, and they rejoiced with her. When they came on the eighth day to circumcise the child, they were going to call him Zechariah after his father, but his mother said in reply, "No. He will be called John." But they answered her, "There is no one among your relatives who has this name." So they made signs, asking his father what he wished him to be called. He asked for a tablet and wrote, "John is his name," and all were amazed. Immediately his mouth was opened, his tongue freed, and he spoke blessing God. Then fear came upon all their neighbors, and all these matters were discussed throughout the hill country of Judea. All who heard these things took them to heart, saying, "What, then, will this child be?" For surely the hand of the Lord was with him. (Luke 1:57–66)

Jesus bore witness that John the Baptist was the greatest man born in the world up to that time. It was his vocation to identify the Messiah. Although John had many disciples, he was not disturbed when they began to leave him one by one and became Jesus' disciples. He had the humility of a truly great man; he was not out to attract people to himself but to bring them to Christ. Jesus manifests a similar movement. He brings everyone to the Father. Divine love gives away everything it has.

John the Baptist seems to have encountered the greatest trial of his life just before his martyrdom. John had been sent by God to point out the Messiah. He had faithfully fulfilled his mission. Now he lies in chains, depressed because of the rigors of that oppression. He had spoken out against the misconduct of Herod, and the king wanted to get rid of him. Lying in chains and separated from his disciples, he had an experience that we, too, encounter in the spiritual journey. It is comforting to know that one of the greatest saints had the same scenario to play out. The dynamic might be called the double bind.

The double bind is not a choice between good and evil but a choice between two goods that seem to be totally opposed, each of which demands our complete acquiescence or commitment. We are also caught in a double bind when two duties seem to be opposed, and there is no way of resolving the dilemma. In the night of sense this takes the form of the "spirit of dizziness" in which we cannot decide what to do. Whenever we try to get advice from a spiritual director or from prayer, we may get a few seconds of peace, and then we are plunged again into the same perplexity.

God uses this tension to move us out of a certain mindset or a certain level of faith to a more mature level of faith. We observe this scenario in the Gospel again and again. Think of the gentleman who asked Jesus to come down and heal his son. He did not have enough faith to believe that Jesus could heal at a distance, so he pleaded with him, "Come down; my son is desperately ill." Jesus said, "I'm not going. You go down."

Immediately that put this man into a dilemma. "Shall I believe in the word of Jesus alone? Can I let go of my mindset? Can he heal without laying hands on someone?" And so he started the long journey. During all this time he was struggling between hanging onto the new level of faith that was so fragile and the temptation to let go of hope and accept the death of his son. As you know, his servants met him on the way and said the boy was healed at the same time that Jesus spoke. This was a tough twenty-four hours. His mindset and cultural conditioning were saying, "It isn't going to work."

A similar thing occurs in our prayer when we know that we have got to pray and at the same time all sense of God's presence has drained out of it and prayer is a mess, just an endless series of wandering thoughts, primitive emotions, and temptations.

We get up saying, "I accomplished nothing. I should have read a book. I shouldn't have bothered with this in the first place." And then the thought comes, "No, I can't give up prayer. I must have committed some terrible fault, but I can't remember what it was." So . . . "Shall I continue the spiritual journey? Shall I give it up?" We can't decide. Sometimes we think yes, sometimes we think no, all the while building up unbearable tension.

One of the classical double binds by means of which God moves us out of our cultural conditioning that limits our response to Christ and our inner freedom is a doubt that threatens the religious convictions we bring with us from childhood, which are not so much matters of faith as the way that we interpret our early religious education. This is where John the Baptist's double bind is so interesting as well as poignant. He was very austere, clothing himself in a loin cloth and eating locusts and honey. He spent years in solitude and silence and then, called by the Spirit, he began his ministry. Jesus himself submitted to his baptism.

When Jesus began preaching, his observance of the Law was more broad. He sat down and had meals with sinners. He did not fast on the approved days, did not limit his preaching to synagogues like the rabbis of his time, but spoke along the roadside and with little reference to scripture. He spoke out of a certain inner authority. He inveighed against the mindsets of the religious leaders of his time.

John's disciples had trouble with Jesus' observance, especially his practice of eating with sinners, which was a no-no for a rabbi. In that culture eating with people was a sign of solidarity or belonging. Eating with sinners suggested identification with them. We need only remember his treatment of the penitent woman and the woman taken in adultery to realize that he was challenging the most cherished religious attitudes of his time.

John's disciples were perplexed. They said to Jesus, "How is it that your disciples don't fast and we do?" This is a familiar question in religious circles, implying our order is better than your order; e.g., we fast more and have longer vigils. Or again, "We Jesuits are better than the Dominicans. We spend a longer time in formation." Or again, "We Protestants are better than Catholics"; or, "We Catholics are better than Protestants." It depends on what side we happen to be on.

Now all this, of course, has nothing to do with religion. It is an expression of the mythical membership level of consciousness that we pass through from age four to eight when we interiorize unquestioningly the values of parents, teachers, and peer groups. In the spiritual journey the Spirit begins to confront the unquestioned presuppositions that are mixed up with genuine religious attitudes. The spiritual journey is a sifting of our motivation and prepackaged value systems by which we judge God, other people, and ourselves.

John's disciples judged that Jesus' disciples did not measure up to their observance of the Law and hence were looking down on them. When John was in prison, he began to remember Jesus' lack of conventional morality, his sharp criticism of the religious authorities, his undermining of accepted attitudes. The parables are like earthquakes underneath people's value systems that are not the values of religion, still less of the Gospel, but are those that have been created by social convention and conformity morality. We don't keep the values of the Gospel because other people do. We keep them because of our personal response to Christ. We are responsible for the way we respond to the Lord and we can't palm off our responsibility on a group, community, church, or anyone else. The call of the Gospel frees us from our preconceived ideas and cultural conditioning and calls us into the freedom of friendship with God, in which we have to decide what we are going to do in relation to social custom and the baggage we bring from early childhood. The Gospel is a call to inner freedom. A fully responsible human self is the first step toward divine transformation.

John's commitment to austerity as the proper response to God may have made it difficult for him to understand Jesus and the latter's preference for mercy over austerity and people over the Law. For John, this doubt seems to have turned into a terrible double bind. "Did I make a mistake? Could this Jesus with his disregard of custom and the Law really be the Son of God? If he isn't, should I acknowledge that I made a mistake? Should I tell my disciples this is not the lamb of God after all?"

Judas had a similar problem but from a different perspective. Jesus did not turn out to be the political revolutionary that he had been hoping for. Jesus was a revolutionary in a much more profound sense. Judas couldn't handle his disillusionment and did away with himself. John could handle it. He sent his disciples to Jesus saying, "Are you the Messiah or should we look for somebody else?" The question manifests the terrible dilemma he was in. "Was I mistaken in pointing you out as the Messiah?" At that time, the Gospel says, Jesus worked a number of the precise miracles that Isaiah had predicted the Messiah would perform. Jesus was saying in the way that wisdom teachers often do, by gesture rather than by word, "You did not make a mistake. I am the Messiah."

The fruit of the double bind catapults us to a new level of consciousness. The dilemma on the level of reasoning is not resolved because it can't be resolved on that level. From the higher perspective the question is simply withdrawn. Reason cannot answer the great questions of life; it can only see that there is not a contradiction in the higher wisdom. The tension, confusion, and anguish of the double bind may be the only way God has of immobilizing the limitations of our preconceived ideas and cultural conditioning. We can then walk away from the mindsets of our particular peer group, family, and early religious education, into the freedom of the Gospel. Jesus did not fit John's idea of the Messiah. John had to find this out and accept it in order to enter into the fullness of his redemption.

Jesus experienced the double bind in the Garden of Gethsemane. He knew that he was the Son of God. And yet the Father was asking him to become sin. The chalice that he was being asked to drink was the feeling of total alienation from the Father. As a human being, he could not put those two together. That is why he sweat blood. The double bind was resolved by his resurrection, ascension, and glorification in which his human nature came to participate in all the divine prerogatives.

The double bind is a liberation, but it feels like the end of our world, including sometimes, the end of our relationship with God. It is rather the end of our *idea* of God. Since God transcends all our ideas, we do not lose anything — except ourselves.

30

THE HOLY MOUNTAIN

After six days Jesus took Peter, James, and John his brother, and led them up a high mountain by themselves. And he was trans- figured before them; his face shone like the sun and his clothes became white as light. And behold, Moses and Elijah appeared to them, conversing with him. Then Peter said to Jesus in reply, "Lord, it is good that we are here. If you wish, I will make three tents here, one for you, one for Moses, and one for Elijah." While he was still speaking, behold, a bright cloud cast a shadow over them, then from the cloud came a voice that said, "This is my beloved Son, with whom I am well pleased; listen to him." When the disciples heard this, they fell prostrate and were very much afraid. But Jesus came and touched them, saying, "Rise, and do not be afraid." And when the disciples raised their eyes, they saw no one else but Jesus alone.

As they were coming down from the mountain, Jesus charged them, "Do not tell the vision to anyone until the Son of Man has been raised from the dead." (Matthew 17:1–9)

Jesus' going up the mountain to be transfigured points to the transformation that we receive on the spiritual journey after a time of purification. After enduring the inner desert of purification, God refreshes us with transforming experiences. The mountain of the Transfiguration is not just a place of retreat. It symbolizes the ex- perience of spiritual awakening that is the purpose of the practice of contemplative prayer.

The first clear indication that contemplative prayer is becoming established in oneself is the attraction to solitude. This attraction comes from the refining of our faculties through the dismantling of our emotional programs for happiness and the consequent reduction of the static that they cause as everyday life keeps frustrating them. In this event the emotional programs of the three apostles have been left on the plain, so to speak, at least temporarily. Their attraction to solitude is symbolized by Jesus leading them up the mountain. It is the first sign of their spiritual awakening.

We begin to access the mystery of God's presence through a similar attraction, even though the particular mountain we are on — a retreat or our daily period of prayer — may not bring us any satisfaction whatsoever. Like an irresistible magnet, the attraction for solitude draws us without our knowing where it is coming from. We wait patiently upon God day after day in prayer and stumble along in our ordinary occupations. The divine attractiveness compels us to continue our climb even when, because of the uneven ground and steep incline, we keep slipping back and have to start the ascent over and over again.

On this holy mountain, Jesus exploded into a presence that overwhelmed the disciples. Every mountaintop or retreat does not provide this experience, but it is a distinct possibility. The divine presence may reveal itself with various levels of intensity.

Jesus turned into light; even his clothes became saturated with it. A kind of glory suffused itself into their senses both inward and outward. If we perceive the divine presence in some facsimile to this clarity, we are fascinated, absorbed, and delighted. Peter's response was to want to stay there forever. The more profound the experience of union, the more one cannot help but wish to prolong it. Peter's idea was to build three tents so that Jesus, the prophets, and the apostles (especially himself) could stay there permanently. He lost all interest in returning to the plain, even though he had a fishing business down there.

Just as the disciples are beginning to experience the delight of the divine presence in the person of Jesus, a cloud suddenly overshadows them. The cloud is the symbol of the unknowing that

we enter as a habitual state through the regular practice of contemplative prayer. Suddenly a voice from the cloud resounded,
saying, "This is my beloved Son, listen to him." Listen not just to
his words to which they had been listening when they were on
the plain, but "listen to *him*," the divine person who is speaking to
you. Listen to the divine presence that is incarnate in this human
being. Listen to the infinite Silence out of which the incarnate Word
emerges and to which it returns.

The voice from the cloud was terrifying to them, a warning to
us that what is revealed in silence on the mountaintop is a min-
gling of delight and confusion, of consolation and desolation, of
reassurance and awesomeness. After all, the voice is the voice of
Ultimate Reality. How does one respond to that?

The response of the three disciples was to flatten themselves
on the ground. When the divine communication is strong, or when
the voice points to something within ourselves that is hard to face,
we too are flattened, disconcerted, confused, not knowing which
way to turn. As the apostles lay there trembling, the voice from
the cloud resounding in their inmost being, Jesus came closer and
touched them saying, "Do not be afraid."

The touch of Jesus, so often recorded in the Gospels, is not a pat
on the back. It is a divine communication. In this instance, it was the
sign of inner healing and symbolized the further development of
spiritual attentiveness beyond the attraction to solitude. It imparted
a new and more profound awareness of the divine presence.

The touch of Christ is like an interior embrace in which
one's fears disappear in an instant. You may be in great distress,
bombarded by disturbing thoughts, overwhelmed by primitive
emotions. You feel that you cannot continue to pray for another
moment! But somehow you say, "I'll wait just one more minute."
Or perhaps you even bring yourself to say, "I'll accept whatever
comes." All of a sudden, out of nowhere, comes the interior touch
of Jesus; his loving hand caresses your heart as if to say, "What are
you worried about?" There are no spoken words as such. What is
communicated is the certitude that God has been there all along,
just hiding; or waiting for us on a different level of our awareness. It was only our habitual level of consciousness from which

he had withdrawn in order to invite us to a deeper experience of his presence.

Notice that the disciples, after he touched them, "saw no one but Jesus." This observation describes the fruit of the interior touch of the Spirit now that the human hands of Jesus are no longer available. The hands of Jesus manifest themselves in the gifts of the Holy Spirit, which lead and move us in varied directions according to the will of the Spirit.

The fruit of the touch of Jesus is to see him in everything that happens. Thus, as the disciples return to the plain, they take with them, not the experience of Jesus' glory, which was so consoling, but something even more valuable: the transformation of consciousness that is the result of their experience on the mountain. Through the touch of Jesus they moved beyond fear and the domination of any emotion and are now able to live life on the plain in union with God. They can live in the market place from their inmost center, their true Self, from the space to which that touch has brought and established them.

The grace of the Transfiguration is not just a vision of glory, an isolated experience of divine consolation, however exalted. Of course, such an experience has immense value. But its primary purpose is something greater: to empower us to live in the presence of God and to see the radiance of that presence in all events, people, the cosmos, and in ourselves.

On the way down the mountain Jesus said, "Do not tell anybody about this until the Son of Man has risen from the dead." There would be no point of talking about it because no one on the plain would understand unless they had climbed a similar mountain. But Jesus may also be hinting that even the gift of divine touch is not the end of the journey. There remains the experience of spiritual taste. Taste arises from taking nourishment into our bodies and transforming it into our own flesh. Thus, it symbolizes the most intimate experience of God — the presence of God as part of ordinary consciousness.

Since Jesus at this time had not yet risen from the dead, it was not appropriate to reveal the interior taste of divine wisdom, which perceives God even in the death of the Son of God on the cross.

This is the grace of Pentecost. It was fitting, therefore, that Jesus hold in abeyance the experience of spiritual taste until the coming of the Spirit. The awakening of spiritual attentiveness, initiated by the attraction to the solitude of the mountain and developed by the experience of Jesus' touch, was completed by the total assimilation of the apostles into Christ's glorified body through the grace of Pentecost.

31

SLEEPERS, AWAKE!

About eight days after he said this, he took Peter, John, and James and went up the mountain to pray. While he was praying his face changed in appearance and his clothing became dazzling white. And behold, two men were conversing with him, Moses and Elijah, who appeared in glory and spoke of his exodus that he was going to accomplish in Jerusalem. Peter and his companions had been overcome by sleep, but becoming fully awake, they saw his glory and the two men standing with him. As they were about to part from him, Peter said to Jesus, "Master, it is good that we are here; let us make three tents, one for you, one for Moses, and one for Elijah." But he did not know what he was saying. While he was still speaking, a cloud came and cast a shadow over them, and they became frightened when they entered the cloud. Then from the cloud came a voice that said, "This is my chosen Son; listen to him." After the voice had spoken, Jesus was found alone. They fell silent and did not at that time tell anyone what they had seen. (Luke 9:28–36)

Let us consider the context of this glorification of Jesus' body. It seems that an inner light that was normally hidden emerged and grew so bright that it saturated his clothes and produced an extraordinary radiance. The divine person of the Word is the source of this light. Jesus miraculously hid this light during his earthly lifetime. We must see the Transfiguration as Jesus' normal state of being since there was nothing inherent to his humanity to limit his glory. Like Moses, who had to veil his face after he came down from the Mount of Sinai because his face had become so radiant that none of the Israelites dared to look at him, Jesus had to veil the presence of the divine Person within his humanity. Faith penetrates this veil and touches the Eternal Word. The disciples were finally ready. This was the moment when Jesus was able to be himself.

Remember how, in the Gospel story of Mary and Martha, Mary of Bethany sat at Jesus' feet in complete, undivided attention. As she listened to his word at this ever-deepening level, she was penetrating the details of his humanity and opening to the divine Person who possessed it. This is precisely what we do in contemplative prayer. We let go of the contents of our rational faculties and the limitations of their ways of knowing. Our awareness slips between the cracks of thinking, feeling, and perceiving and fastens on the person of Christ. Jesus' words to the Samaritan woman, "I who speak to you am he," invite us to see Christ in every person and indeed in every event. The cosmos is the body of Christ in varied forms of expression. As faith grows, the disguises of God fall away and we perceive the divine presence and its activity within and around us all the time.

Thus this incident is an instruction in contemplative prayer and its fruits in daily life. Having enjoyed this awakening of faith, the apostles returned to the plain, "seeing Jesus only," words that refer to the perception of the divine presence everywhere.

For the three disciples the Transfiguration was just one experience. Its special grace did not establish them in an abiding state of God-consciousness. But it was clearly a decisive event in their lives. Once we realize that this text is a mirror reflecting what is taking place in us through contemplative prayer, it also becomes a decisive event in our lives.

"Jesus took Peter, James, and John and led them up a mountain to pray." They did not take themselves. In contemplative prayer we may have the sense of being carried or led by the hand, or even of being thrust into this experience.

The mountain represents a place apart, freedom from the cares and preoccupations of the plain, which represents everyday life. In coming into a retreat atmosphere, we, too, are in a place apart. It may be that God has waited a long time to get us into this particular location, time, and company. We might have received the same grace in other situations. But God often chooses circumstances that are just right to impress upon us a special grace.

"Peter and those with him had fallen into a deep sleep." This sleep refers not to somnolence, but to the deep rest of contemplation, the rest that is the result of letting go of our ordinary stream of consciousness with its particular contents. We move beyond thoughts, feelings, and sense perceptions and are led by the Spirit into the solitude of our inmost being.

Notice that the apostles fell into a deep sleep. It was the rest that comes from profound absorption and self-forgetfulness, signs that one has withdrawn from the external senses and even, temporarily at least, from the false self. In this rest, when everything is quiet, we become nonreflective, and our awareness rests in the divine presence. This presence is without particularities; it is simply present. The deep rest associated with it bonds us with God and prepares us for God's transforming communications. It also leads to a direct encounter with the unconscious.

This encounter can take place in two ways. One is the jettisoning of the repressed emotional material of our personal history. This is the work of the dark nights that bring the false self to an end. We are led to the truth about ourselves: to the recognition of the dark side of our personality, our mixed motivation, and the emotional damage of a lifetime. The other form of encounter with the unconscious refers to the releasing of spiritual energies that have been repressed in the course of the development of the false self.

Having enjoyed the deep sleep of contemplation, the disciples woke up. "Awakening" is a key word in the contemplative understanding of the Gospel. One of the fruits of awakening is a heightened spiritual perception. Hence, "they saw his glory and the two men who were standing with him." The delight in seeing Jesus' glory bathed the disciples inwardly as well as outwardly and left them with the eager desire to prolong their enjoyment. Peter expressed his desire in the words, "Lord, it is good to be here!" Who would not want to stay on the mountain of Transfiguration? It is easy to say, "Be detached from divine consolation," but the more intense the enjoyment, the harder it is to return to the ordinary course of life.

Peter "didn't really know what he was saying." He was just expressing his exuberance. While he was still speaking, "a cloud came and overshadowed them." This indicates the deeper communication that was now possible because of the bonding with God that took place in the deep sleep of contemplation. "Overshadowing" is a key word in scripture for the most profound experiences. Solomon and the entire congregation were overshadowed by the cloud that filled the Temple on the occasion of its dedication. Mary, the mother of Jesus, was overshadowed by the Holy Spirit at the annunciation.

From the cloud came a voice that said, "This is my chosen one; listen to him." Here is a divine encounter similar to Jesus' words to the Samaritan woman at the well in the Gospel of John. In her case, the intensity of the experience was veiled by Jesus' humanity. Here there is the immediate perception of the divine presence reducing the false self to silence.

As the disciples lay on the ground, Jesus approached and touched them, banishing their fears. It is characteristic of divine communications to create a certain awe in the beginning, but they quickly become reassuring and consoling. The unexpectedness and profundity of such an encounter catch one's security system unawares and it registers fright. But then the divine touch places a great big kiss, so to speak, in the middle of one's spirit and an immense sweetness flows through all the senses and faculties, establishing them in profound peace.

Having been reassured by Jesus, the disciples descended the mountain and returned to everyday life, bringing with them this contemplative perspective. Once the divine presence has been established as part of their ordinary reality, they perceive the divine person in Jesus and find God in everything.

In similar fashion, contemplative prayer awakens us to the consciousness of Christ within us and to his personal experience of Ultimate Reality as Abba, the God of infinite compassion, concern, and caring for every living thing.

32

RESTING IN GOD

After six days Jesus took Peter, James, and John and led them up a high mountain apart by themselves. And he was transfigured before them, and his clothes became dazzling white, such as no fuller on earth could bleach them. Then Elijah appeared to them along with Moses, and they were conversing with Jesus. Then Peter said to Jesus in reply, "Rabbi, it is good that we are here! Let us make three tents: one for you, one for Moses, and one for Elijah." He hardly knew what to say, they were so terrified. Then a cloud came, casting a shadow over them; then from the cloud came a voice, "This is my beloved Son. Listen to him." Suddenly, looking around, they no longer saw anyone but Jesus alone with them. (Mark 9:2–8)

The Feast of the Transfiguration is celebrated in the church on August 6, but the Transfiguration Gospel is also read on the Second Sunday of Lent. In the context of Lent this text follows the temptation of Jesus in the wilderness, indicating that all ascetical practice, desert experiences, and penances are a preparation for transfiguration. The experience of God (the transmission of the divine consciousness) is given in the degree that we are prepared to receive it. The period of Jesus in the wilderness followed his baptism in the Jordan where he seems to have been anointed by the Holy Spirit with the full consciousness of his divine personhood, as well as of his mission. The Spirit led him into the wilderness; he, in turn, led the disciples up this high mountain.

At the river Jordan, the voice from the cloud said, "This is my beloved Son on whom my favor rests." The Spirit descended in the form of a dove and rested upon him. Rest is the sign of divine transmission. It is the interior milieu in which we move toward complete openness to God's presence and action within. It means that we participate in the descent of the Spirit upon Jesus. His consciousness of the Ultimate Reality as Abba, the God of infinite compassion, is extended to us.

In the context of Christ's anointing by the Spirit and his extension of that anointing to each of us, the experience on the holy mountain is of great significance. The practice of contemplative prayer opens us to the gentle but firm invasion of truth, light, and love.

The experience of the disciples is a paradigm of the awakening of spiritual attentiveness. The first sign of this development is called by Fathers of the Church "the divine perfume." Perfume is an analogy of the sweetness of the divine presence. The divine presence, like pleasurable objects to the external senses, is attractive. The attraction of the external senses obviously is different from that of the inner experience of grace that draws us to our inmost center. There is no reflection, no effort, no activity on our part. The attraction rises up because the divine presence is there. As soon as the obstacles that keep it hidden in ordinary life have been sufficiently reduced, the divine perfume slips through the cracks of our defense mechanisms, and a whiff of the sweetness of God's presence is experienced. It is an attraction to something within us that we had not known before, at least not in this degree. God lifts a corner of the veil and the aroma of the divine sweetness escapes. Like the perfume in the house of Simon, which filled the whole house, the divine presence fills our entire being with its delight. The awakening to this presence is signified in this event by Jesus leading the disciples up the high mountain. Even when our time of prayer is a mess, unbearable, boring, going nowhere, this mysterious anointing will not let us go. On some level we feel the attraction for silence, solitude, prayer, and the need to be faithful to the practice.

Christ calls to us throughout all time, "Come to me all you who labor and are burdened and I will give you rest." "Rest" refers to interior quiet, tranquility, the peace of the abyss, the rootedness of being one with the divine presence.

"Rest" implies that we are beginning to experience the mind of Christ, his awareness of the Godhead as infinite mercy, concern for everything that is, and the servant of creation. This rest is our reassurance at the deepest level that everything is okay. The ultimate freedom is to rest in God in suffering as well as in joy. God was just as present to Jesus in his abandonment on the cross as on the mountain of Transfiguration.

The sense of spiritual touch is a more intimate experience of the awakening of spiritual attentiveness. We observe the frequent reference to touch in Jesus' miracles. He touched little children and put his arms around them. This hugging of children symbolizes the interior embrace of God in which we are not just attracted to the divine presence, but are in immediate proximity to it. Jesus touched the hand of Peter's mother-in-law and the daughter of Jairus, and they stood up. The touch of Jesus initiates the process of inner resurrection. It imparts health at every level of our being.

Jesus offers his most sublime teaching at the Last Supper through the symbol of taste. The Eucharist effects a union with God that transcends the senses; it is the inner penetration of spirits. It leads to the consciousness that can say, "The Father and I are one." This oneness is symbolized by transforming the bread and wine into our own flesh and blood. It is the pledge that God wills to enter into every aspect of our life, even our cellular structure, and, by becoming one with us, to take us totally into himself.

33

THE RESOLUTION OF OPPOSITES

After six days Jesus took Peter, James, and John and led them up a high mountain apart by themselves. And he was transfigured before them, and his clothes became dazzling white, such as no fuller on earth could bleach them. Then Elijah appeared to them along with Moses, and they were conversing with Jesus. Then Peter said to Jesus in reply, "Rabbi, it is good that we are here! Let us make three tents: one for you, one for Moses, and one for Elijah." He hardly knew what to say, they were so terrified. Then a cloud came, casting a shadow over them; then from the cloud came a voice, "This is my beloved Son. Listen to him." Suddenly, looking around, they no longer saw anyone but Jesus alone with them. (Mark 9:2–8)

The liturgy this morning is communicating to us one of the peak experiences recorded in the Gospel. The celebration of spiritual consolation is intended at this moment of Lent to communicate to us the insight that the path of repentance, temptation, and inner purification leads to inner resurrection and transformation. On this occasion the disciples were led apart to this great solitude on the top of the mountain and saw Jesus turned into light. Their senses, minds, and spirits were flooded with the glory imparted from the body of Jesus as his divine glory suffused his person and diffused its power and beauty into their awareness. Throughout the ages of church history this event is regarded as a paradigm and a transmission of the grace of contemplation. The disciples were established in a new awareness of the divine presence in themselves, in Jesus, and in all creation.

The liturgy then invites us this morning to the heights of joy and consolation. The news of current events,* on the other hand, plunges us into an ocean of grief. If you watch the television reports, you daily perceive sights, if not the smell, of death. The news provokes feelings of profound sorrow for the loss of life, dismay at the destruction of the environment, and worry in regard to the future consequences of such a mammoth tragedy. Thus, we find ourselves this morning in an extraordinary situation and challenge. We are confronted at the same moment by the heights of spiritual attainment and the depths of the human condition in one of its darkest hours. How do you put together such a height and such a depth?

In the first lesson this morning, we read about Abraham's willingness to sacrifice what was dearest to him, his beloved son. At the last moment, God provided a substitute and accepted the will for the deed, pouring out on Abraham all the consolations that are symbolized in the experience of the three apostles on Mount Tabor.

In the second reading, Paul points out that this situation was repeated in the person of Jesus when he sacrificed himself for the Father; only in his case there was no substitute. He died! He was God's only begotten and beloved Son. God did not rescue him at the last moment as he did Abraham. God's representative at the cross was Mary, the mother of Jesus. She must have felt the same kind of feelings that Abraham felt on that lonely, windswept mountaintop. God did not provide a substitute for her. Her son died in the utmost agony and abandonment. Those of you who have been praying and working for peace have a special relationship to God this morning. There is no substitute for your sacrifice, just as there was no substitute for Jesus' sacrifice. One meaning of this morning's confrontation with these abysmal opposites is the awareness that whatever your disappointment,

---

* This homily was given on Sunday, February 24, 1991, the day after the beginning of the ground offensive in the Persian Gulf War.

a special identification with Christ's passion and death belongs to you.

The fact that there was no substitute for Jesus' sacrifice tells us something about God. God is vulnerability. That is the message of the cross. God does not save himself. God does not protect himself.

We don't know this God! Christ has tried to open a window onto what the Ultimate Reality is like. Human reason collapses in front of a God who by all the standards of human reason is foolishness itself. God goes on forgiving us day after day and we go right on sinning. Forgiveness just does not work. But God does not stop forgiving. God goes on, endlessly making the same (from the human viewpcint) mistake. We forgive a little, bit by bit, but not like this.

This vulnerability of God opens a window that may lead us to some understanding of the world of opposites. God is total solidarity with the oppressed, the afflicted, the suffering, and the poor. Such is his revelation in the Old and New Testaments, and it is epitomized in Jesus' teaching and example. This means that violence, war, and torture are not just injuring people; they are tearing God to pieces. That is why violence is so terrible. It is not just we who are involved; God is totally involved with people and their suffering. That is why even if there is some just reason for violent self-defense, it never changes the fact that it is God who is dying, so to speak, in the victims of violence; God who is torn to pieces; God who, through identification with creation, is suffering in them. Thus the resolution of opposites in some way is linked to whom or what God is: total vulnerability. Paul says, "The foolishness of God is wiser than the wisdom of people."

Why are people so fragile? So vulnerable? So broken? So pitifully weak? Falling again and again, doing the most dreadful things, needing to be endlessly forgiven. Maybe it is because God is so vulnerable, at least in the sense that he is touched by the slightest sign of good will (see the Book of Jonah, especially the last few verses).

The height of consolation and the depth of desolation, of death and resurrection, raise the ultimate questions. Death isn't going to go away, and the glory of the resurrection is still a promise. Human reason is unable to resolve the ultimate opposites. But if we accept the opposites and come to rest in them, we may go to a new level of reality in which the question itself is not answered, but simply withdrawn.